ART BOOKS

FROM CRESCENT MOON PUBLISHING

Leonardo da Vinci
by James Pearson

Early Netherlandish Painting
by Rosalind Mutter

Piero della Francesca
by Naomi Haskell

Giovanni Bellini
by Julia Davis

Fra Angelico: Art and Religion in the Renaissance
by Rosalind Mutter

Eric Gill: Nuptials of God
by Anthony Hoyland

Minimal Art and Artists in the 1960s and After
by Laura Garrard

Postwar Art
by George Knighton

Vincent van Gogh: Visionary Landscapes
by Stuart Morris

Max Beckmann
by Stuart Morris

Egon Schiele: Sex and Death in Purple Stockings
by D. Simon Eade

Mark Rothko: The Art of Transcendence
by Julia Davis

Jasper Johns: Painting By Numbers
by L.M. Poole

Brice Marden
by Laura Garrard

Frank Stella: From Minimalism to Maximalism
by James Pearson

GIOVANNI BELLINI

GIOVANNI BELLINI

Julia Davis

CRESCENT MOON

CRESCENT MOON PUBLISHING
P.O. Box 393
Maidstone
Kent, ME14 5XU
United Kingdom

First published 1994. Second edition 2008.
© Julia Davis 2008.

Printed and bound in Great Britain.
Set in Bodoni Book 10 on 14pt.
Designed by Radiance Graphics.

British Library Cataloguing in Publication data

Davis, Julia
Giovanni Bellini
I. Title
759.5

ISBN 1-86171-164-5
ISBN-13 9781861711649

Contents

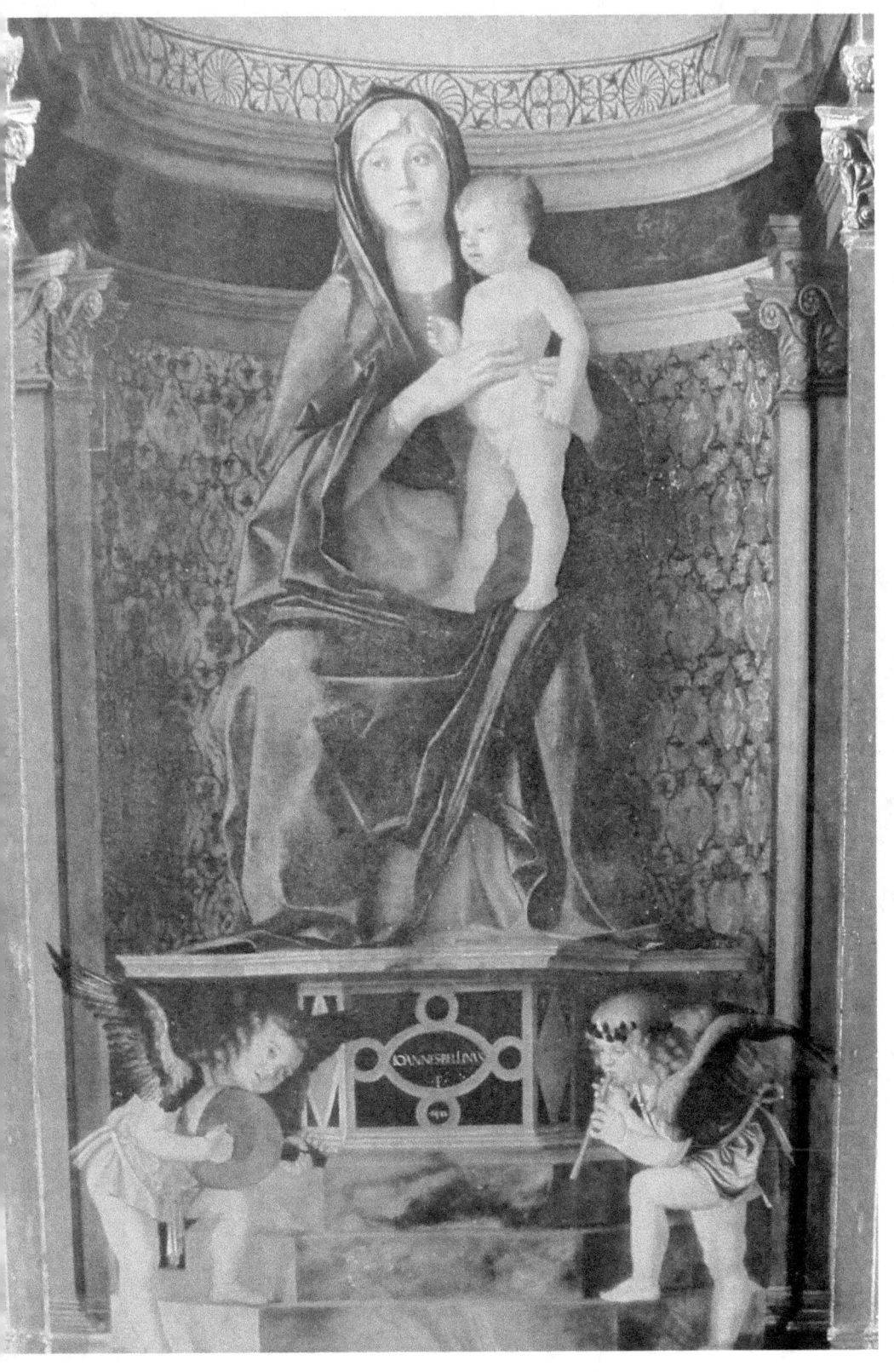

Giovanni Bellini, Madonna and Child Enthroned, 1488, Venice

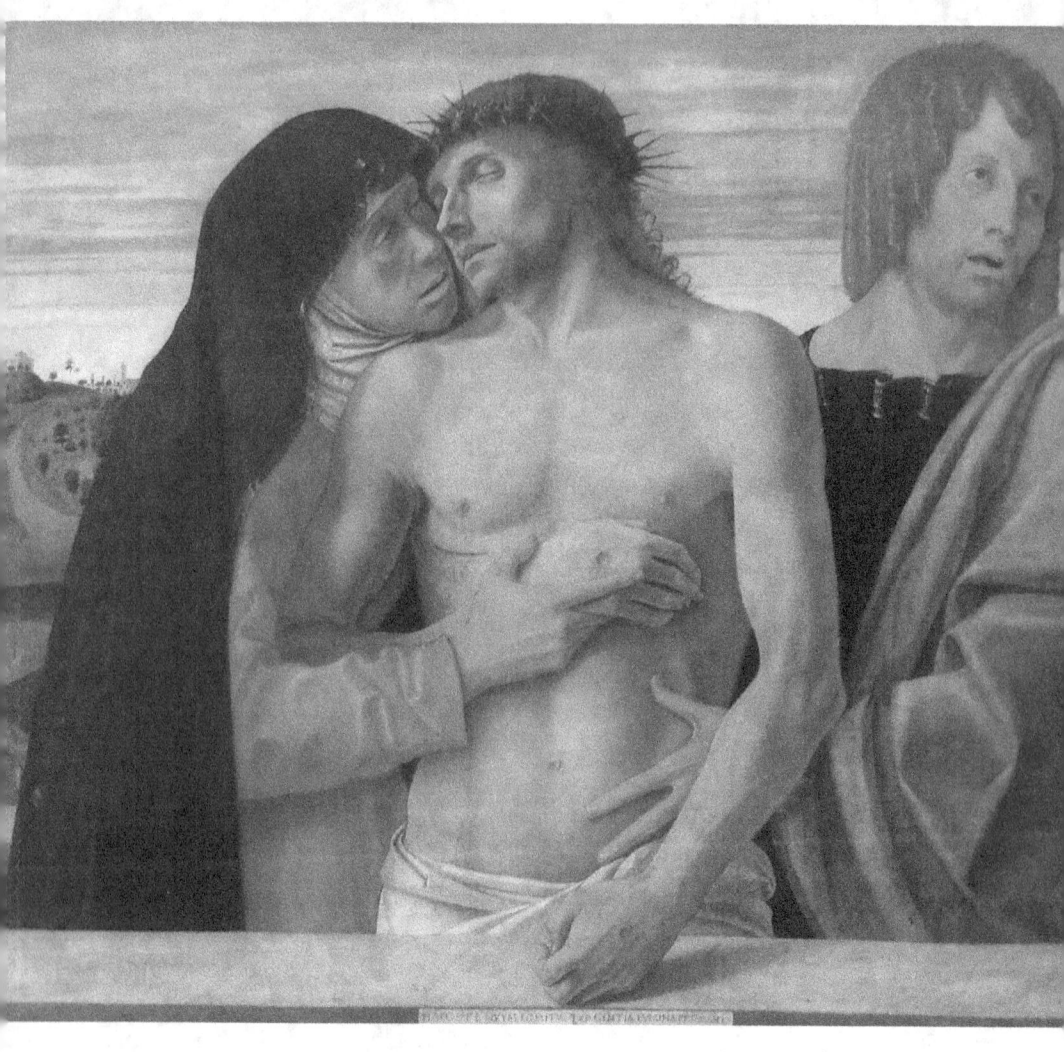

Giovanni Bellini, Pietà, Milan

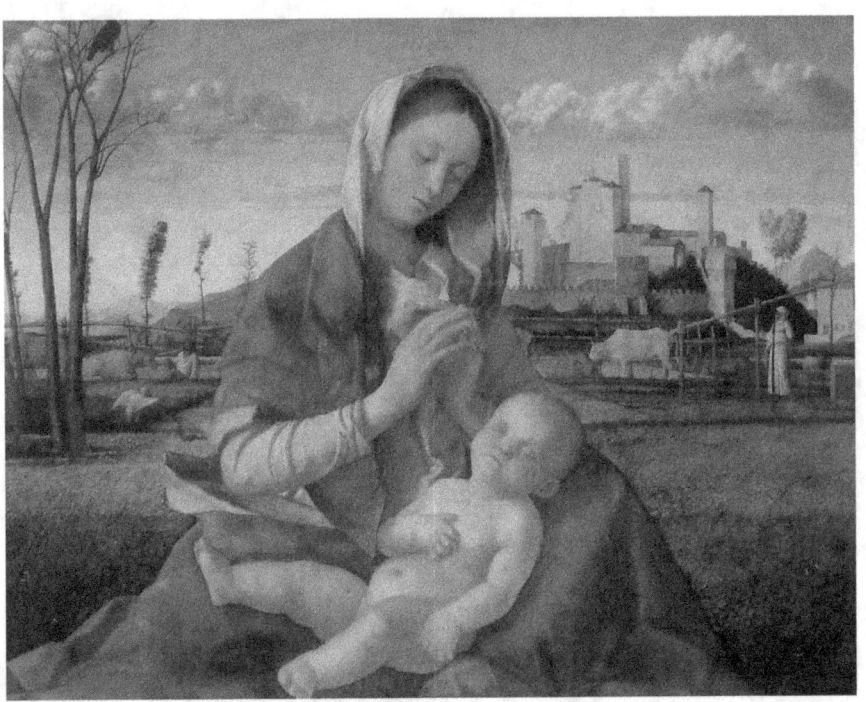

Giovanni Bellini, Madonna of the Meadow,
National Gallery, London

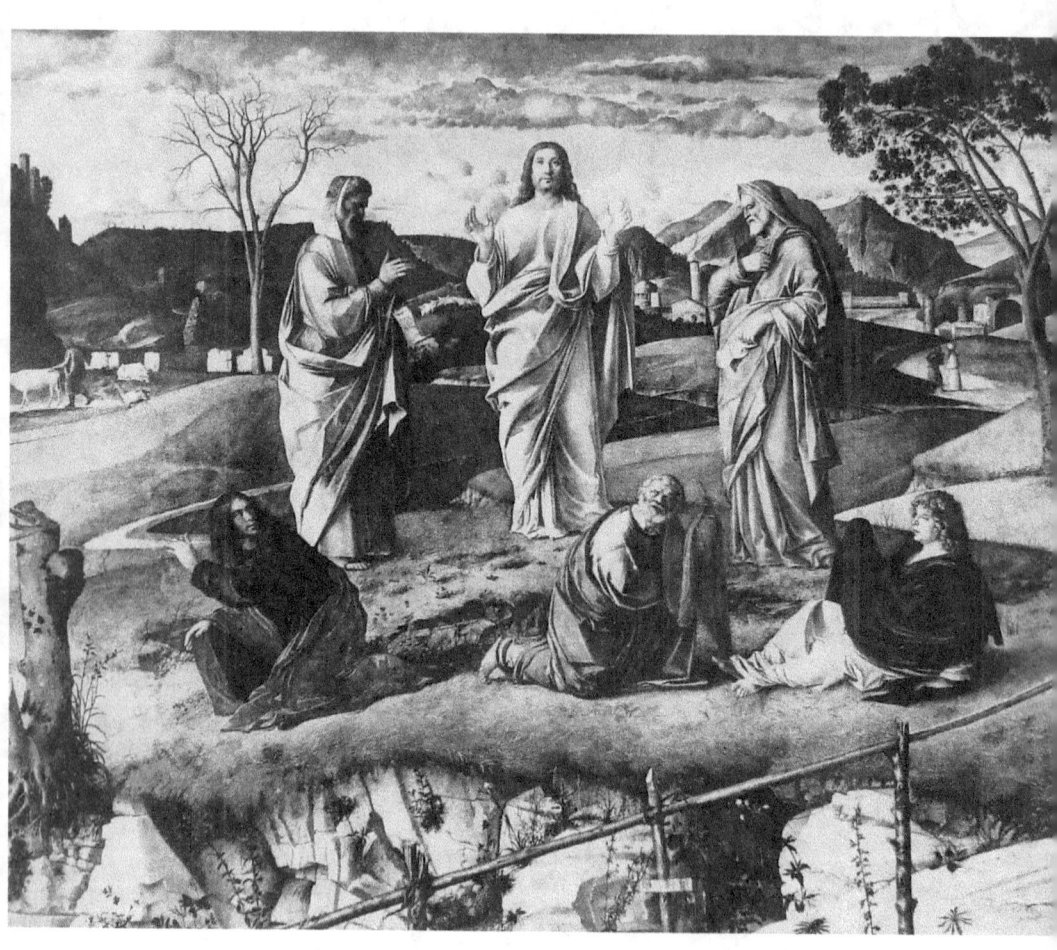

Giovanni Bellini, The Transfiguration, 1485-90

1

Introduction

Giovanni Bellini has highly praised me before many nobles. He wanted to have something of mine, and himself came to me and asked me to paint him something of mine, and said he would pay well for it. And all men tell me what a God-fearing man he is, so that I am well-disposed toward him from the outset. He is very old, but is still the best painter of them all.

Albrecht Dürer[1]

Giovanni Bellini (*c*. 1430-1516) is the author of some of the most exquisite of Renaissance paintings. He is, in a sense, the painter's painter, who had a long career, like his pupil, Titian, of painting. He influenced many artists, among them Titian, Giorgione, Vecchio, Sebastiano del Piombo, and Dürer. His influences include Mantegna, his father, Jacopo Bellini, Antonello, and Donatello.

Bellini does everything in his paintings that Renaissance painters are supposed to do: he painted beautiful pictures, devotional images, of the Madonna, Christ and various saints; he painted mythological scenes, and scenes from history; he refined and defined Early Renaissance space, bringing it into the High Renaissance; he inaugurated a new feeling for landscape; he remained true to the sacred and emotional aspect of painting to the end of his career; he developed the various formats of Renaissance painting – the small, private devotional pictures, the large, public altarpieces, a host of secular portraits and large-scale friezes.

On the one hand you might see Bellini's art as being entirely based in the Quattrocento:

> although Bellini continued to paint until his death in 1516, [writes Rona Goffen] he remained mired in the quattrocento, responsive to the new art of these young masters but unable or unwilling to assimilate their innovations.[2]

At the same time, one might see Bellini as supremely a high Renaissance artist, especially in his later altarpieces, where his sense of space seems in tune with Titian or Raphael.

Bellini's style is very sweet. His paintings are full of a love for painting, and a love for his subjects. The ambiguities in his works do not arise from his intentions, which are, as with so many Renaissance painters, to be as exalting as possible. So his Madonnas and saints are lovingly painted.

The German poet Rainer Maria Rilke, like so many poets, went to Italy and found it overwhelming beautiful: in letters to his Muse, Lou Andreas-Salomé, Rilke spoke of the 'painted God in gold' skies of Florence, the wild roses along the white gravelled paths, the 'gentle Madonnas' in the galleries.

Of Venice, Rilke said that being there as the 'golden dome' on the 'palace of heavenly treasures' of his holiday. The 'stone fairy tale' of Venice' utterly enchanted him.[3] Rilke's response to Venice is typical of so many other writers and poets. It is out of this exquisite city that Bellini's art comes.

There is an undeniable sensuality in Bellini's art. Central to his art is his sensuality. It is the same with the art of Leonardo, Caravaggio, Titian, Vermeer, Rembrandt, and Rubens. The sensuality of the paintings themselves, as objects, is crucial to their evaluation æsthetic-ally. Bellini is a sensual painter – not simply in his treatment of eroticism, or in the eroticism of his forms, but also because he painted self-consciously erotic subjects. He painted female nudes: the *Woman with a Mirror* (in Vienna), in *The Feast of the Gods* (in Washington) and in the *restollo* of *Truth* (in Venice).

Bellini's sacred art is as erotic as his secular art, as with any painter. Indeed, one might say that some of Bellini's Christian paintings are more erotic than his paintings of mythological or historical subjects. His *Pietàs*, for instance, with that lovingly described dead, nude Christ, may be seen as more erotic than the Classical scenes. The eroticism of art depends a lot on the viewer's response. And on painterly surface and technique. Erotic art may defined as simply 'æstheticized sexual representation' (L. Nead, 103).

In Bellini's art, as in the work of Titian and Leonardo, the sensuality of the paint surface is primary in the 'genius' of the art, in the critical acclaim the art generates. Frank Stella, the American abstract painter, writes of Caravaggio's sensuality in *Working Space*:

> The second miracle of Caravaggio is the miracle of surface. Skin, flesh, and pigment blend into reality. Painting is acknowledged as an act and as a physical fact, but immediately afterward, almost simultaneously, the presence of the human figure is felt as real, touchably there. (1)

Bellini's painterly talent looks forward to the voluptuous outings of Titian, while Titian's soft colouring, his blurring of forms, his use of luminous lighting and his open use of paint look towards Impressionism and modern painting.

Bellini is very much a central artist in the Western 'high art' tradition, like Leonardo, Raphael, Michelangelo, Titian, Tintoretto, Poussin, Ingres, Turner and Manet.

The sensuality of the artist's sense of touch is crucial to the 'greatness' of art, as Lynda Nead writes:

> the artist's subjectivity that is registered by the brushwork and surface is sexualized. Art criticism writes sex into descriptions of paint, surface and forms. (58)

The critics who consider and write of Bellini do this. And when you think of the great 'high art' critics – Berenson, Burckhardt, Clark, Ruskin, Pater, Warburg, Gombrich – they have all exalted the *jouissance* of painting.

Paul Gauguin wrote of the sensual primacy of painting in the familiar terms of late 19th century 'theory of correspondences', which was used by many poets, painters and dramatists:[4]

> Painting is the most beautiful of all arts. In it, all sensations are condensed...
> A complete art which sums up all the others and completes them. – Like
> music, it acts on the soul through the intermediary senses: harmonious
> colours correspond to the harmonies of sounds.

Other artists have spoken lovingly of the loving nature of the canvas itself, the beauty of the art object. Maurice Denis wrote: 'The emotion – bitter or sweet, "literary" as the painters say – emerges from the canvas itself, a plane surface covered with colours.'[5]

2

Colour

Bellini's colours are bright but soft. There are few harsh shadows. He uses precise, graphic lines, like Andrea Mantegna, but much softer colour. Bellini's colours are generally warm. There is a glow, a luminosity in Bellini's paintings that is not rare in Renaissance painting, but few painters are as warm as Bellini. There is a golden warmth in Stephan Lochner's magnificent *Madonna in the Rosegarden* (in Cologne), in many of Fra Angelico's *Madonnas* (the Turin *Virgin and Child*, for instance), in Mantegna's *Presentation in the Temple* (in Berlin), in Titian's late *Pietà* (Galleria dell' Accademia, Venice), and in Joos van Cleve's *The Rest on the Flight into Egypt* (Brussels). But Bellini produces his own golden glow which is quite different from any other Renaissance painter. It is part of his artistic 'signature', you might say.

In the *Madonna and Child in the Madonna dell 'Orto* in Venice, warm colours overpower the austerity of the Virgin's dark blue cloak. The patron who ordered the painting said:

I want and order that the painting of Our Lady made by the hand of Giovanni

Bellini...be framed in a carved and gilded frame and made as beautiful and sumptuous as possible...[6]

The Madonna and Child is indeed a rich and sumptuous painting: the cloth of honour behind the Madonna is richly embroidered; and the Madonna wears a bright red dress, this time quite visible under her cloak.

In the portraits, Bellini shows just how good he was at painting skies: the quarter-length figures are often shown against nothing but skies. A balcony is before them, and that is the only architecture or furniture in the picture. *The Portrait of a Young Senator* (Padua), *Portrait of a Patrician* (Rome) and *Portrait of a Patrician* (Uffizi), *Portrait of a Man* ("Pietro Bembo") in London depict men against a soft blue sky. Bellini makes these skies a speciality. They are always cloudy, populated by wispy white clouds, the clouds of a windy day. It is often late in the day in Bellini's paintings: the sky is overcast, and there is often a strip of yellow glowing on the horizon. Bellini's skies reveal just how closely he had studied Nature. We see skies like this everywhere, these half-overcast, half-sunny half-cloudy skies. Skies such as that found in *The Baptism of Christ*, in Venice, where God presides over storm clouds, but beyond is a pale strip of cerulean sky, and beyond that the glow of golden clouds. These skies flourished later on in the Arcadian vistas of Claude Lorraine and Poussin.

Critics draw attention to the 'luminosity' of Bellini's paintings, to use Julia Kristeva's term. Rona Goffen writes of the *San Giobbe Altarpiece* thus: 'Bellini's San Marco seems filled with golden light and air.' (153) The *San Giobbe Altarpiece* is bathed in a soft, Autumnal light, the glow of ripe apples, perhaps. It is also a Byzantine gold, which connotes, as in Byzantine icons, divinity. In Bellini's art, the gradual change from the gold background of Byzantine and Trecento painting to the blue sky of the Quattrocento is complete.

Some of Bellini's Madonnas are arranged against nothing else but cerulean coloured sky (the *Frizzoni Madonna*, for example, in the Civico Museo Correr, Venice, or the Philadelphia *Madonna and Child*, which is perhaps autograph, perhaps a copy). The gold of Heaven in Byzantine icons becomes the blue of the sky in Renaissance art. Of course, the

Madonna wears the sky on her body, as C.G. Jung notes;[7] the connections between the Madonna and azure goes back a long way – to ancient Goddesses such as Isis, to the notion of the Night, the Milky Way, as a Goddess.[8] Madonna blue persisted for a long time in Western art,[9] and azure was of course an expensive pigment (indeed, it was as expensive as gold). Bellini's paintings are full of this rich blue: the *Brera Madonna*, the *Madonna Greca*, the *San Zaccaria Altarpiece*, Bellini's last great altarpiece of the Blessed Mother of God.

In the *San Zaccaria Altarpiece*, which John Ruskin called one of the two best paintings in the world, the opulence is suggested by the saturation of the colours in the costumes. Gold is present in the capitals of the pillars, and in the mosaic in the semi-dome. At the centre, the colours of the Madonna's robes dominate the painting: the crimson and the blue is the richest there is. In terms of pure colour, only painters such as Titian created such pure and deep colours. Bellini's colours recall the purity of Trecento and early Quattrocento colours, where blues and reds were pure blues and reds, and had little or no other colours added to them, as in Simone Martini's *The Entombment* (Berlin).

Although he paints shadows in the clothes of the Madonna and various saints and figures, Bellini keeps his colours undiluted, so that in each of the costumes – the patriarch's red robes in the *San Zaccaria Altarpiece*, for instance – we find only red and dark red, that is, red mixed occasionally with black. Bellini's colours are, then, naturalistic, as the description of the spacious, airy apse in this painting shows, but he retains a symbolic sense of colour for particular, special elements in a picture. His colours are always rich when they need to be. By holding back the other colours in a painting – in the *Madonna of the Meadow*, for example – Bellini allows himself room to make opulent statements in rich, saturated colours in the holy figures. The exquisite pale azure sky in the *Madonna of the Meadow* is transcended in intensity by the blueness of the Virgin's cloak. In Bellini's paintings, saturation of naturalistic colour does the work of gold in Byzantine icons: to emphasize the specialness of divinity.

The punched and patterned gold of Early Renaissance and Trecento art becomes the æthereal azure of the sky, and of the Virgin's cloak.

Even as Renaissance art became increasingly 'realistic', with its illusions of three-dimensional space, it did not lose its 'unreality', its idealistic views of divinity, its idealizations of life.[10]

3

Space

Space…is eternal and indescribable… provides a position for everything that comes to be, and…is apprehended without the senses by a sort of spurious reasoning and so is hard to believe in – we look at it indeed in a kind of dream and say that everything that exists must be somewhere and occupy some space, and that what is nowhere in heaven or earth is nothing at all.

Plato, *Timaeus*[11]

Frank Stella writes of the space a painting creates, and how this space can envelop the viewer, sensually:

An effective painting should present its space in such a way as to include both viewer and maker each with his own space intact. It is not that this experience should be literal; it is simply that the sense of space projected by the painting should seem expansive: expansive enough to include the viewing and the creation of that space. (*Working Space*, 9)

Giovanni Bellini's sense of space is highly refined. It is quite different from the spatial mysticism of Piero della Francesca. Piero's planes of light and airy volumes dissect space in terms of mathematics made mystical. In Piero, perspective and proportion fuse with religious adoration to produce a timelessness, lambent art. In Fra Angelico, space is flattened, with few hints at volume. In Botticelli, space is secondary to the blissfulness of line, shape and contour. Botticelli's spaces are essentially flat and, like Angelico's bright and shadowless. In Masaccio, space begins to open up from the spaceless golden backgrounds of Byzantine art.

The *Crucifixion* from Masaccio's *Pisa Altarpiece* (in Naples) depicts four figures (Jesus and the 'three Marys') against a gold background which suggests, as gold always does in Renaissance painting, power an divinity. With the *Trinity* (in Santa Maria Novella, Florence), Masaccio's space deepens. The evocation of the architecture in Masaccio's *Trinity* is very powerful. He creates a barrel vault between two pilasters, seen from a low viewpoint. The architectonics of the *Trinity* are showy, theatrical, like a stage. Masaccio monumentalizes his subjects, making God the apex of that strongest of all geometric shapes, the triangle or pyramid.

Giovanni Bellini, in his large altarpieces, uses a monumental sense of architectonics, following on from Masaccio. Bellini's sense of space is deep, and, in the Quattrocento, few painters are as deep, spatially, as Bellini. Leonardo is deep, of course. But then, no one is deeper, in every sense (culturally, psychologically, æsthetically), than Leonardo. Bellini pushes space back and further back, until, by the time of the *San Giobbe Altarpiece*, it is the fully-rounded, three-dimensional illusionistic space of the Renaissance, and of all painting subsequent to the Renaissance. Bellini's sense of space is that 3-D illusionistic space that is the basic space of all post-Renaissance art. James Beck writes:

Renaissance painting remains the basis of all subsequent Western art despite the shattering innovations of the past hundred years. (9)

This statement might seem a little strong for people who look at abstract art; people who say, hold on, what about Malevich's black squares, isn't that a big departure from Renaissance painting? Or Mark Rothko's cloud-like, transcendent canvases? Or Donald Judd serial 'sculptures'? Or Alison Wilding's abstract objects? In one sense, contemporary art is, as James Beck says, founded on Renaissance art, and Renaissance space.

Bellini's contribution was to make the development from Quattrocento flatness to High Renaissance space complete. In the *San Giobbe Altarpiece* and the *San Zaccharia Altarpiece*, in particular, the architecture rises monumentally above the figures, not dwarfing them, but providing a suitably magnificent setting for the picture's religiosity to be apparent. As in the art of Andrea del Sarto or Pontormo, or any of the Renaissance religious painters, architecture is part of the overall spiritualization of the painting.

Bellini uses architecture for spiritual purposes, as with any other Renaissance religious painter. For him, architecture plays a part in the overall spiritualization of a painting. That is, architecture is spiritual space, it is the symbolization or manifestation of spiritual feelings.

We are always aware of architectonics in Bellini – he never lets the viewer forget the significance of architecture. Like Piero della Francesca, Bellini realizes religious emotion in terms of space. He has, like Piero, a heightened sense of space, and the possibilities of spatial dynamics.

The magnificent frames help to create a sense of space, too. The frames of Bellini's paintings are particularly grand. True, many, if not most, Renaissance paintings were elaborately framed. The frame around Bellini's *Baptism of Christ*, in the Garzadori Chapel of St John the Baptist, Santa Corona in Vicenza, is gigantic, and is a work of art in itself. People talk about 'church furniture', and paintings are seen as part of the 'furniture' of the church. Paintings were seen, in the Middle Ages and in Renaissance times, as precious objects in themselves. When monasteries or churches commissioned works from painters, they usually stipulated what materials were to be used, and how much they would cost. The patrons and commissioners of Renaissance art were concerned about the physical quality of the works: the richer the materials (azure, gold, expensive pigments) the richer the spiritual quality of the work. The physical and the spiritual became interconnected, æsthetically. In Bellini, as in so many of Renaissance painters' art, the painting as an object helps to extend the space of the church, illusionistically.

Giovanni Bellini uses deep tones, quite unlike Piero or Botticelli. There is a darkness to Bellini's painterly technique which has affinities with the Early Netherlandish painters (van Eyck, Roger, Memling, Massys, David). Even though they employ dark tones at times, the Quattrocento painters (Masaccio, Angelico, Masolino, Pisanello, Gentile, Sassetta, Domenico), these are really dark colours. The result is still lightness and airiness.

In Early Netherlandish painting of the same period (say, 1400-1450), there is a darkness which produces rounded forms: in Robert Campin's *Madonna* (London), or Roger van der Weyden's *Madonna and Child Standing in a Niche* (Vienna) or Jan van Eyck's *Madonna of Chancellor Rolin* of *c.* 1435. Bellini strives for such sculptural volumes, and he achieves it, with his late altarpieces. In these paintings, the sense of illusion is paramount, for the paintings aim to be visual extensions of the interior of the church. As with *trompe l'oeil* ceilings of the Baroque era, the aim is to produce the illusion that the spectator is in the same space as the holy figures. Sacred and secular merge: the viewer is included in the same 'working space' of the painting, as Frank Stella suggests.

The viewpoint in the *San Giobbe Altarpiece,* the *San Giovanni Crisostomo Altarpiece,* and the *San Zaccaria Altarpiece* is low: the viewer approaches the painting as if s/he's approaching the actual space depicted in the painting. James Beck writes of the *San Giobbe Altarpiece* thus:

> The low horizon relates the painted figures to us, the spectators, since the fictive space seems to flow naturally from outside the frame. Bellini's approach to modelling differs from that of Mantegna, Piero, and Antonello because he increasingly forgoes the edges of his forms. Rather than drawing the outside surface and then filling in the modelled parts from the silhouette, he modelled with light and shadow from the inner core outward, gradually arriving at the contours. (245)

Turn a corner in a church in Venice, and there is the Blessed Mother of God, with Christ on her lap, surrounded by various saints. She is right there, right in the Venetian church. This is the effect Bellini desired. In the Renaissance, and especially in the Byzantine era, an *image* of the Madonna was believed to be, in some way, the Madonna herself. That is, there was not such a great divide between illusion and 'reality' as there is today. People of old, it is said, believed in the miraculous properties of paintings. Paintings were magical objects in their own right. This is obvious with famous paintings such as the *Mona Lisa*, which was causing a stir in Leonardo's studio way before he had even finished it. Bellini's aim is also religious: to paint the Virgin Mary *as if she were actually there,* in front of the viewer. The more 'realistic' the likeness, the greater the painter, so it was believed in the Renaissance.

Vasari often enthusiastically gushes about the lifelike qualities of this or that painter in his *Lives.* Lifelikeness was revered, as it is still is today. Bellini, then, like Leonardo, achieved a sublime sense of lifelikeness in Quattrocento art. With painters such as Perugino, Verrocchio and Leonardo, Bellini appears as the most 'lifelike' or naturalistic of artists. At the same time, though, his paintings are 'unreal', and idealized, and quite unnatural. For, even as he strives after naturalistic, imitative effects, he will put something in a picture that is clearly metaphorical, or allegorical, some incident in the background of a painting (like the snake and bird behind the Virgin in the *Madonna of the Meadow*). Or he will put one of those cloths of honour behind the Virgin, and show no way of supporting it, as in the *Brera Madonna.*

Side by side with this naturalism of late Quattrocento painting, then, there is an extreme unreality and idealism. For all the naturalism of the meadow and the little hill town in Bellini's *Madonna of the Meadow*, so delicately depicted, the situation of the Madonna sitting with her eyes closed and a naked god on her lap is supremely unreal.

One aspect of his sacred paintings that Giovanni Bellini made his own was the parapet or balcony, seen at the bottom of so many *Madonna and Child* and *Pietà* paintings. The parapet helps to define the illusion of space. Often the Child is resting on it, the Madonna huge behind him, her arms around him, as in *Madonna and Blessing Child,* (Venice), and the *Lochis Madonna* (Bergamo), or, as in the *Davis Madonna*, she watches him sleep on the parapet.

Many of Bellini's paintings are formulaic, depicting the same elements, juggled about occasionally, in painting after painting. The parapet is a device he uses to frame the figures. It also suggests an elevated space, the roof or balcony of a building perhaps, giving a reason for the marvellous views of the landscape behind Jesus or Mary. The ledge is usually marble, a material which add suitable gravitas to religious paintings.

Further, the parapet suggests an altar, quite appropriate in religious art. For Bellini's small *Madonnas*, like his *Pietàs*, were devotional paintings, made for private use. The suggestion of an altar brings the sense of the church into the domestic interior. In the devotional *Pietàs*, the slab of marble serves to suggest the tomb, in Bellini's many depictions of the dead Christ in the tomb, a format popular in the late mediæval era, the *Imagio Pietatis*. The small devotional paintings enabled the presence of the Madonna or Jesus to enter one's own room. There was a continuity between church and home, and the link was the visual image. The ledge, parapet or balcony in Bellini's small paintings linked the inner, illusionistic space of the painting with the outer, 'real' space of the home. One could, it seems, lean on that parapet, and be in the same space as the Madonna herself. The parapet, like Bellini's other illusionistic devices, enabled the painting to throw a 'working space' around the viewer.

Another aspect of Bellini's sense of space is central to his art: the hanging cloth, the 'cloth of honour'. 'Cloths of honour' had already appeared in Early Netherlandish art – the beautiful green, gold and red patterned canopies and hangings in Jan van Eyck's *Lucca Madonna* (Frankfurt), *The Madonna of the Fountain* (Antwerp), and *The Virgin and Child with Saints and a Donor* (New York), and in Roger van der Weyden's marvellous *St Luke Painting the Virgin* (Boston) and *The Virgin and Child Standing in a Niche* (Vienna).

It forms the major part of the background of paintings such as the famous *Madonna Greca* (in Milan), the *Madonna of the Pear* (Bergamo) and *The Virgin and Child* in New York. As Rona Goffen writes, the 'cloth of honour' 'pushes the sacred figures forward, toward the picture plane' (43).

Bellini's Madonnas are very close to the picture plane, close enough to touch. The parapet is not a distancing device, rather it brings the Madonna and Child or dead Christ forward. The 'cloth of honour' helps to focus attention on the figures, as in the Fort Worth *Madonna and Child*, the *Morelli Madonna* (Bergamo), the *Madonna degli Albereti*, and the Detroit *Madonna of the Blessing Child* (painted by Bellini with assistants).

The hangings are opulent in paintings such as *Votive Painting of Doge Agostino Barbarigo* (Murano): a beautiful red 'cloth of honour', creased so elegantly, is edged with gold, is edged with gold, contrasting pleasingly with the green baldachin. The luxuriance of such hangings was also explored by other Renaissance artists such as Sebastiano del Piombo, Raphael, Andrea del Sarto and Jacopo Pontormo, but it was undoubtedly Caravaggio who painted the richest cloths and hangings (in, for instance, his *The Death of the Virgin*, in the Louvre, or his *The Madonna of the Rosary*, in the Kunsthistorisches Museum, Vienna, where a huge red cloth is tied around a pillar).

In Bellini's *Brera Madonna*, the cloth is green, but no support for it is indicated. It simply hangs there. The Madonna sits before it and – unusually in Bellini – looks directly at the viewer, as does the bambino. As with the *Madonna of the Meadow*, the Virgin is and is not sitting in the landscape. The green silk hanging adds to the separation of Madonna from landscape.

The throne functions to emphasis the weight of divinity in Renaissance paintings, and Bellini, like Angelico and Mantegna, paints many thrones upon which the Madonna sits. The most opulent throne in Bellini's *œuvre* is undoubtedly the marble-encrusted throne in the *Pesaro Altarpiece*, although the thrones in the other altarpieces are also suitably majestic.

The throne, like the rest of the architecture in Renaissance art, screams power. In some Renaissance paintings, the Madonna is enthroned very high above her subjects. In Giorgione's enthroned *Madonna with Saints Francis and Liberale* (Church of San Liberale, Castelfranco Veneto), the Virgin is raised seven or so feet above the saints. There are no steps up to this high throne: one imagines she floated there.

In Bellini's art the throne sits squarely in the centre of the painting. Bellini employs simple geometry and proportion in his paintings. In the small *Madonnas*, she is placed centrally, the hanging and parapet framing her squarely. In the later altarpieces, pyramidal structures predominate, again with the Madonna at the apex. She is the figure of power and divinity. Only rarely in Renaissance is God the Father actually shown, standing behind Jesus, Mary, the saints and angels. God appears at the back of Masaccio's *Trinity*, and he's sometimes glimpsed in the corner of *Annunciations*, throwing down a dove to Mary, but it is rare to see him in Renaissance art. If Jesus or Mary are in the painting, God usually isn't. When you do see God, it's a surprise, as if he shouldn't be there: he looks awkward, out of place.

4

Landscape

Giovanni Bellini is undeniably one of the great early landscape painters of the Western tradition. His landscapes are marked by precise lines, bold designs, minute details, a meteorological accuracy, a fondness for outcrops of rocks and for scudding clouds.

We have seen landscapes before in Early Renaissance art – in the background of Fra Angelico's *Annunciations*, a few flowers, or in Angelico's *Descent From the Cross*, a subject that lends itself to a landscape treatment, or in Giotto's *Lamentation*, or in Uccello's various *Battle of San Romano* paintings. But in these painters, the landscape is still very much a background, flattened spatially, so the action in the foreground is not connected with it. Early Renaissance landscape is full of marvellous passages of detail and light, but it is flat and relatively undynamic. The background of Giotto's *Lamentation*, where the weeping angels swarm like crazed birds, the landscape is hardly painted in: the suggestions of rocks, a tree, and that's about it. Samuel Beckett used this landscape – the barren, rocky space inhabited by a single, twisted,

Alberto Giacometti-like tree, in his *Waiting for Godot.*

With Bellini's paintings, landscape begins to come alive. Clouds, for instance, appear, and suggest skies in which real airs blow and breathe. Bellini loves rocky spaces, barren, dusty, where the rocks are incredibly precisely depicted, every crease or crevice, every fold of soil and edge of rock. The blasted trees are scrawny and leafless, as in the London *Agony in the Garden* or *The Resurrection of Christ.* When trees do have leaves, as in *The Transfiguration* (Naples), every leaf is painted, as with Claude Lorraine in his Arcadian pastoral landscapes.

In Bellini's art, as in other Renaissance painters, landscape is symbolic, so the backgrounds or landscapes in which Christian scenes occur are aligned to the spiritual content of the image. Bellini's landscapes are spiritual, part of the Christian theme or subject of his paintings. The barren, stony, dusty spaces of Renaissance Christian paintings are the visual equivalent of the harsh, ascetic teachings of Christianity. The last days of Christ typically take place in hard, stony places – the agony in the garden, the Crucifixion on the hill, the burial and resurrection at the sepulchre.

Bellini's landscapes, like those of Giotto, Masaccio, Angelico and Lippi are fully in tune with this ascetic, sparse spiritual imagery. Rona Goffen writes of Bellini's spiritual landscapes thus:

> ...for Bellini, sky and landscape were more than compositional devices and metaphors: he made them the causation of his style, the logical explanation of his colorism, and, more than this, the affective determinant of the psychology of his images – hence the emotion of the beholder. (104)

Bellini's spiritual landscapes, in his *Agony in the Garden, St Francis in Ecstasy* (New York), and *Sacred Allegory (Meditation on the Passion)* in the Uffizi in Firenze, are beautifully evoked spaces. Bellini paints the cusp or borderland between the wilderness and the city. He does not site his figures in a wholly wild landscape. There is always human life in the background. If not people going about their business – a man driving a donkey, two people talking, a man on horseback – then some accurately drawn town. Behind most Renaissance painting, whether Netherlandish or High Italian Renaissance, there is some town in the background. It may be some idealized Græco-Roman city (as in the art of Botticelli or Perugino), or, as in the work of Bellini and Piero della Francesca, a provincial Italian village or small town. Even in the background of *St Jerome in the Desert*, which one would imagine is a subject that calls for a humanless wilderness, there is a town (in the predella of the *Pesaro Altarpiece*). Even in the most austere depiction of St Jerome in the wilderness, Leonardo's tormented, unfinished painting, there is a city, indicated in the top right hand corner.

Bellini poeticizes his towns. They are not wholly accurate, 'realist' renditions of particular places. They are part of his overall spiritualization of Nature. For Bellini, as for Angelico or Raphael, Nature is the creation of God, so everything in Bellini signifies some spiritual feeling.

The city in the background of so many Renaissance landscapes signifies culture, the presence of culture in Nature. Even in the countryside, seemingly uncontrolled by people, there are always people. So, the city is always there, in the background of the Renaissance painting.

Bellini explores the relation between inside and outside, between inner, psychological space and outer, public space. Some of his paintings, such as the luminous *Madonna in the Meadow*, deliberately play with notion of foreground and background. The Madonna in this painting dominates foreground and background. She is a pyramid, precisely centred, at the apex and core of the world evoked in this painting. Her blue dress spills over the bottom edge of the painting, so it appears she is and is not sitting in the field. Despite the pastoral elements of the *Madonna in the Meadow* – cattle, a farm, peasants – it is a sombre picture. The trees, for instance, have few leaves left on them. Or at least, the trees nearest the Virgin have been stripped of their leaves. Again and again, we see the tree in *Madonna and Child* paintings looking forward towards the Cross. The symbolic links between trees and Christ's Cross are well-known. Piero della Francesca's great fresco cycle in Arezzo celebrates the passages of the 'true Cross' from the days of Adam to Jesus. The deeper meaning of the symbolic identification of the Cross and the tree is feminine. The tree is Nature, and Christ is crucified on Nature, on Mother Nature. The Cross is the maternal presence: Christ is crucified on the body of his Mother.

Throughout Renaissance painting, the Mother is primary: the central image is the Mother nursing her Child. At the Crucifixion, the other most popular Renaissance image, the Mother is present, watching her son's death. Sometimes the 'three Marys' are depicted. But the Madonna is present in another way: she is the wooden Cross upon which he writhes in agony. The Madonna has always been central to Renaissance religious painting: she is not only central to Renaissance religious painting, she is at the *visual* centre of most Renaissance paintings. She is the focus of the paintings. She sits on a throne, or stands, and is at the centre. The Child sits slightly to one side. The Virgin is central.

It is the same with depictions of the Crucifixion: the Cross is central, and the Cross is the Mother, symbolically (as well as symbolizing other things). Jesus sits on his Mother's lap, just as Horus sits on the lap of the Egyptian Goddess Isis. At his death, too, Jesus rests on the body of his Mother.

This mystery – of the present/ absent Mother – is found throughout Bellini's paintings.

5

The Altarpiece

In the early polyptychs of the Renaissance, the Madonna and Child were in the centre panel (obviously), with various saints in the side panels, separated by golden pillars, as in Giotto's *Baroncelli Polyptych* (Giotto and workshop, Santa Croce, Florence). The hierarchy of divine power was also indicated by relative scale, as in Duccio's marvellous red and gold *Maestà* in Siena), where the Virgin dominates the gathering of saints and luminaries by being twice their size. The polyptych allowed for a compartmentalization of power and importance in a painting. With the *sacra conversazione*, the figures were into a single, unified architectural space. The golden wooden pillars separating each panel were left out (Fra Filippo Lippi painted thin his *Barbadori Altarpiece*, in the Louvre, establishing an uneasy relation between the painterly scene of the painting and its relation to the frame). Domenico Veneziano painted columns in his *St Lucy Altarpiece* (Uffizi) to indicate power relations.

Bellini, in his altarpieces, developed the the *sacra conversazione* space, although in some altarpieces, such as the *Frari Triptych*, he used the pillars of the frame to separate the figures in his painting. Jacob Burckhardt called this painting 'Probably the most perfect work of this whole type to be executed in the fifteenth century' (60).

The typical Bellini space is the apse of a church, as we have said, as also in Alvise Vivarini's Berlin altarpiece (*Virgin and Child with Saints*, formerly Kaiser-Friedrich-Museum, Berlin (destroyed 1945). Vivarini's *Virgin and Child*, though, is much grander, more showy than Bellini's apses. Jacob Burckhardt wrote in his *The Altarpiece in Renaissance Italy*:

> More than elsewhere in the fifteenth century, Renaissance architecture is conceived here as a beautifully proportioned space, and as an appropriately sacred setting for the ideal existence of the various holy figures. (73)

Piero della Francesca had painted a magnificent vision of an apse, in his *Brera (Montefeltro) Altarpiece*, where the complex composition is set alight by that single, hanging white egg. Other painters employed the barrel-vaulted apse of a church as the background for their Madonna paintings – Raphael in his *Madonna del Baldacchino* (Uffizi), Ercole de' Roberti in his *Virgin and Child with Saints* (Milan), Botticelli in his *St Barnabas Altarpiece* (Uffizi).

The church apse is a framing device, a symbolic device, but also an opportunity for the painter to show off her/ his talent for devising spectacular displays of perspective. Bellini is no exception to this: his apses are certainly spectacular, the most flamboyant being perhaps the *San Zaccharia Altarpiece*, which allows for a slither of landscape on either side, and the familiar Bellini clouds and pale blue sky. Andreas Mantegna had exploded the staid monumentality of the apse setting in his *Madonna della Vittoria* (in the Louvre), with its bower of fruit and leaves and birds.

6

Sacra Conversazione

In Giovanni Bellini's altarpieces, the *sacra conversazione* is played out, as it is in all Renaissance *sacra conversazione*, in complete silence. These are 'sacred conversations' in which there is no conversation. No one says anything: no one looks at anyone else. Take Bellini's *San Zaccharia Altarpiece*: the Virgin, as ever in Bellini (and most Renaissance painters) looks down, sad, mute (she is 'caught in the grips of primal repression', as Kristeva puts it); the Saints Lucy and Catherine of Alexandria stand either side of the Madonna on the throne, also looking down; Peter and Jerome flank them, looking down also, lost in thought. The result is a silent interplay of contemplation; each figure muses in their own space, connected visually but not emotionally to the other figures.

This is very apparent in many *sacra conversazione* paintings: the *distance* between one person and the next, despite their physical proximity. In many *Virgin and Child with Saints* paintings, as the *sacra conversazione* images are often titled, we find this melancholy meditation suffusing the picture: the evocations are of timelessness, as if these figures have been standing or sitting in those poses forever. Nothing moves, no flutter of wind, there is no sound, no crying of children outside the picture, no ill-mannered gestures, nothing uncouth or inappropriate.

The *sacra conversazione* paintings are remarkably silent, motionless paintings, where the paint is smoothed onto the wood panel or canvas without a single ripple, where no external forces disturb the inner calm of the protagonists; where no one shows any emotion other than quiet introspection. After all, the Child sitting on the Madonna's lap is a time for rejoicing, surely? The Child is young, the Madonna is young, but these pictures have an incredible emotional *weight* about them: they are heavy images, full of the weight of death, of sadness, of fate.

The *sacra conversazione* paintings are an impossible situation: the divine appearing in person, on Earth, in a space at once sacred and secular. There sits the Virgin and her child, and the mystery remains total to the end, because she is *divine*, yet she appears on Earth, that is, in a profane realm.

These Renaissance paintings depict, then, the meeting of the impossible (divinity) with the possible (Earth). It is impossible that the Virgin is there at all; it is impossible that she is a *virgin* yet she has a child. Every *Madonna and Child* painting repeats this mystery. For, there she is, a virgin, but with her own child on her knee.

Bellini paints these fusions of the sacred and the secular with a quiet confidence, emphasizing the sensuality of the event, painting so carefully the costumes and faces of the saints and donors. His paintings rehearse the inrush of the sacred, but in the quietest, most thoughtful and circumspect manner.

Bellini's spaces are small, clean, perfect worlds: a balcony or a terrace overlooking some idyllic Italianate landscape, as in the votive painting of *Doge Agostino Barbarigo* (at Murano). Here, the figures stand or kneel or sit in utter silence, in front of a crimson cloth of honour. Angels play music, but you can't hear it. Bellini's paintings are not full of music, like, say, Piero della Francesca's marvellous and sonorous *Nativity*, where the five angels sing loudly. In Bellini's paintings, one imagines the scene to be very quiet, so perhaps distant birds are heard, very faintly, miles away in the pastoral Italian landscape.

Bellini's landscapes are those of sleepy afternoons in late Spring, Summer or early Autumn. They (re)present a sun-warmed world which is both naturalistic and deeply symbolic. Set against the marble steps and green and red hangings, the costumes of the saints and noblemen and divinities in Bellini's pictures stand out brilliantly. All is tranquil harmony in Bellini's paintings, where the sun shines warmly, low in the sky, usually from the left. The figures tirelessly retain their symbolic poses, hands clasping books, swords, staffs and musical instruments. The austerity of the spiritual dimension is offset by the opulence of the costumes and settings.

7

Emotion

Now we come to the emotional content of Giovanni Bellini's paintings. They are sad, very sad. Rarely does a smile appear on anyone's face. There is the insipid half-smile of Saint Sebastian in the *San Giobbe Altarpiece*, but that is a rarity in Bellini's art. Nearly all his people are melancholic: his Madonnas, in particular, are wistful, always looking down, or into the distance, hardly looking at the viewer. Bellini's Virgins seems to be contemplating their fate as the Mother of God. It is the same with Angelico's Madonnas, or those of Botticelli or Titian or Massys. Leonardo da Vinci, it seems, is rare among Renaissance painters giving the Madonna his famous Gioconda Smile. Bellini's Madonna smile, meanwhile, is essentially that of his *Madonna Greca*: holding her child, seemingly in the 'bloom of motherhood', to use a typical cliché, the Virgin looks down, head titled, eyes open but staring, unfocused, into nothing, mouth fixed straight, or, often turning down slightly. Julia Kristeva writes:

> The face of his Madonnas are turned away, intent on something else that

draws their gaze to the side, up above, or nowhere in particular, but never centres it in the baby.[13]

There is not much laughter, humour or even joy in Christianity. Instead of emphasizing the Resurrection of Christ, that joyous bursting back into life after the Crucifixion, it is significant that painters concentrate on the Pietà, the dead Christ, looking pathetic and mournful as he is dragged from the Cross and laid in the tomb. This woeful glorification of suffering is at the heart of the Christian religion. This sad feeling of the *Pietà* painting also suffuses the *Madonna and Child* painting.

You have to ask the Blessed Virgin Mary: why so sad? Why are you so sad? The answer is that she is a masculine creation, the image of male projections, about patriarchal attitudes towards women and motherhood. In Christianity, it seems you can't be seen to smile or laugh when 'great', 'important' emotions are being portrayed. You can't smile and be serious about motherhood; you can't laugh as you ponder death. There are no smiles at the Crucifixion, even though we all know the Son of God ascends after his 'human' death. Similarly, the Madonna is not shown smiling, except in rare cases.

8

Motherhood

Although she is at the heart of Renaissance painting, the Madonna is decentred, psychologically and theologically. Although she is the *Mother* of God, his geneatrix, his womb, his birth, she is decentred, sidelined, displaced.

As Julia Kristeva writes in "Motherhood According to Bellini":

> ...craftsmen of Western art reveal better than anyone else the artist's debt to the maternal body and/ or motherhood's entry into symbolic existence – that is, translibidinal *jouissance*, eroticism taken over by the language of art. Not only is a considerable portion of pictorial art devoted to motherhood, but within this representation itself, from Byzantine iconography to Renaissance humanism and the worship of the body that it initiates, two attitudes toward the maternal body emerge, prefiguring two destinies within the very economy of Western representation. Leonardo Da Vinci and Giovanni Bellini seem to exemplify in the best fashion the opposition between these two attitudes. On the one hand, there is a tilting toward the body as fetish. On the other, a predominance of luminous, chromatic differences beyond and despite corporeal representation. Florence and Venice. Worship of the the figurable, representable man; or integration of the image accomplished in its truthlikeness within the luminous serenity of the unrepresentable.[14]

The treatment of the Madonna is complex in Renaissance painting and in Western religion. She is eroticized, for a start: most, if not all, Renaissance *Madonna and Child* paintings eroticize the Madonna. Yet, at the same time, she is desexualized; the actualities of motherhood are smoothed over. Breast feeding is shown, but the attitude to it is ambivalent, as it is still is today, where people get uptight when they see someone breast feeding 'in public'.[15]

Against science, in the Renaissance, there is religion. The Madonna presides over the religious domain. Julia Kristeva remarks:

> There is *Christian theology* (especially canonical theology); but theology defines maternity only as an impossible elsewhere, a sacred beyond, a vessel of divinity, a spiritual tie with the virginal and committed to assumption.[16]

Indeed, to be so slavishly worshipped, as the Madonna is throughout her history and throughout the Catholic world, from South America to St Petersburg, is not simply positive and enriching. It puts her in a particular position which, understandably, she was probably reluctant to accept. You see this reluctance in the Renaissance paintings of the Annunciation. As Andrea Dworkin writes in her book *Right-Wing Women*, it is not always honey and milk to be worshipped as a Goddess:

> this premise about a biologically based morality is used, the woman-superior model of antifeminism is operating to keep women down, not up, in the crude world of actual human interchange. To stay worshipped, the woman must stay a symbol and she must stay good. She cannot become merely a human in the muck of life, morally flawed and morally struggling, committing acts that have complex, difficult, unpredictable consequences. She must not walk the same streets men do or do the same things or have the same responsibilities. Precisely because she is good, she is unfit to do the same things, unfit to make the same decisions, unfit to resolve the same dilemmas, unfit to undertake the same responsibilities, unfit to exercise the same rights.[17]

Dworkin's ruthless polemic is simplistic: it polarizes notions of masculine and feminine and rides over ambiguities, yet when we apply it to the Virgin Mary, how accurate it seems, in its basic thrust.

The best reading of the psychology of Giovanni Bellini's art is undoubtedly Julia Kristeva's "Motherhood According to Bellini", where Kristeva discusses the portrayal of the maternal body in Bellini's (and Renaissance) art. In Kristeva's reading of Renaissance philosophy, the woman is simultaneously allowed to be and not to be the mother; she is placed centrally and simultaneously decentred; she is exalted by painters even as she is denigrated. Julia Kristeva notes:

> The language of art, too, follows (but differently and more closely) the other aspect of maternal *jouissance*, the sublimation taking place at the very moment of primal repression within the mother's body, arising perhaps unwittingly out of her marginal position. At the intersection of sign and rhythm, of representation and light, of the symbolic and the semiotic, the artist speaks from a place where she is not, where she knows not. (ib, 242)

Present in the painting, the real woman is elsewhere. This is clear when we look at Renaissance Madonnas: the 'real' woman, the flesh and blood, living and breathing woman is elsewhere. She is not in the painting. The painted Madonna is a cipher, a symbol, 'pure figment', as Samuel Beckett says of his Goddess figure in *Ill Seen, Ill Said*. Life is elsewhere said the guru of the Surrealists, André Breton, and in Renaissance paintings, the actual mother is elsewhere. Geoffrey Ashe in his book *The Virgin* calls Mary 'the obscure Jewish wife', remarking that it is amazing that this 'obscure Jewish wife' should become one of the central figures of Western culture, subject of thousands of Renaissance paintings, not to mention mediæval cathedral sculpture.

Any religious painting is an interface between the human the divine, between the secular and the sacred. It is an uneasy, ambiguous relationship. The painting is both a mundane object, a bit of wood, canvas and pigment, purchased in the dusty streets, brought back to the studio, and put together by the painter. The painting-as-object is thoroughly secular, thoroughly ordinary. Yet it is also a sacred object, a piece of magic. The painter works with solid, real materials to create something that is illusion, not very solid, really; the painting is something unreal, insubstantial, ethereal, impossible to grasp, something powerful though; in short, something *magical*.

Painters of all eras wrestle with these physical, semantic, psychological, æsthetic and metaphysical tensions. The tensions between abstraction and representation, between 'illusion' and 'reality', between colour and 'life'. The religious painter has to deal with the ever-impossible task: the depiction of the invisible and the unknown. The artist has to make the ungraspable graspable, as Julia Kristeva notes:

> The artist, as servant of the maternal phallus, displays this always and everywhere unaccomplished art of reproducing bodies and spaces as graspable, masterable objects, within reach of his eye and hand.[18]

Bellini's Madonnas present a *jouissance* of maternal space that is, Kristeva writes, 'beyond discourse, beyond narrative, beyond psychology, beyond lived experience and biography' (247).

Renaissance Madonnas are eroticized through selective parts of the body. We do not see the Virgin naked, ever. We see, in fact, only her face and hands, sometimes her neck. Her body is always covered up. And not just loosely covered, but thickly, heavily covered, heaped up with azure and crimson robes, dresses, wimples and hoods.

Every Renaissance painter had to learn how to paint folds in clothes, and Bellini spends a good deal of time and effort producing deep, shadowy folds, 'the luminous folds and secret depths of the sacred' as Kristeva calls them (260). These folds are themselves part of the overall eroticization of the Virgin, and of motherhood. Unable to paint the *body* of the Mother of God, Renaissance painters threw themselves into painting her face and hands, and her clothes. The Madonna's wardrobe is always rich, always indicative of profusion and luxury. The Blessed Virgin Mary is the mother the painter always wanted: quiet, subdued, passive, nurturing, enfolding the child in swathes of love and connection, symbolized by the arms and hands around the child, and those luxuriant robes. Bellini concentrated on creating luminous folds, with deep shadows – in his *Frari Altarpiece,* for instance, or in the *Madonna and Child with Saints and Donor* (in Düsseldorf).

The folds in the Virgin's mantle are a way of painting the power of the Virgin without revealing her body, the body which has to be absent, as Julia Kristeva writes:

The image of the Virgin – the woman whose entire body is an emptiness through which the paternal word is conveyed – had remarkably subsumed the maternal "abject," which is so necessarily intrapsychic.[19]

Julia Kristeva reads Bellini's art as a secret autobiography in which the artist tried to displace the the father and site himself within the maternal body, to 'rewrite' the body of the mother in his own fashion.

> Giovanni wanted to surpass his father, within the very space of the lost-unrepresentable-forbidden *jouissance* of a hidden mother, seducing the child through a lack of being... He aspired to become the very space where father and mother meet... Bellini penetrates through the being and language of the father to position himself in the place where the mother could have been reached. He thus makes evident this always-already past conditional of the maternal function, which stands instead of the *jouissance* of both sexes. A kind of incest is then committed, a kind of possession of the mother, which provides motherhood, that mute border, with a language; although in doing so, he deprives it of any right to a real existence (there is nothing "feminist" in Bellini's action), he does accord it a symbolic status. (in ib., 248-9)

Not 'feminist', then, Bellini's paintings in fact uphold every stereotype of 'woman' and 'motherhood' you care to imagine. In fact, Bellini does not question stereotypes at all: he maintains them. He depicts the Madonna as the drudge of humanity, the drudge as Goddess. Bellini's Madonna is really a mask, too, of something that remains always out-of-reach. The Madonna, as Kristeva notes, 'increasingly appears as a *module*, a process' (ib., 264).

> Nowhere else but here, it seems [Kristeva writes], in the luminous folds and secret depths of the sacred that painting strives to capture; with regard to it, the myth of the maternal figure is nothing but a screen, a foreground, or an obstruction to be broken through. (in ib., 260)

Joseph Campbell speaks of the 'masks of God', and Bellini's paintings are like Russian icons, objects that point beyond themselves, to some mystery beyond. The 'mystery beyond' is that Other, the primal mother, the space Bellini (and no artist) can ever fully grasp.

9

Pain

There is little pain in Giovanni Bellini's painterly style. The world he creates is relatively painless, compared to the world of, say, Mathias Grünewald or Roger van der Weyden. There is nothing as gruesome or as painful as Grünewald's *The Isenheim Altarpiece* in Bellini's output. Michael Levey writes: 'Bellini 's world is intensely stable... His faith is sure, and his reason quite effortlessly follows it.'[20]

There is pain in Bellini's paintings, but it is heavily stylized, as in Raphael or Andrea del Sarto. In one of Bellini's most celebrated works, the *San Giobbe Altarpiece*, that hero of martyrdom, St Sebastian, stands quite calmly, with half a smile on his face, nearly naked, with an arrow in his belly and one in his calf. He stands in a daydream, as if he might be thinking of some glowing incident in his childhood. Meanwhile, he has two arrows stuck in him, and he bleeds. Such is the strangeness of the Renaissance (i.e. all Western art), that this image of pain can be presented as something quite serene.

Painters throughout Western history have reflected the violent acts of Christianity, portraying them as heroic gestures, heroic gestures made sublime by the stylization of 'high art': Botticelli painted the massacre of the Innocents; Poussin depicted St Erasmus having his entrails pulled out by a winch; many painters portrayed St Sebastian full of arrows (Mantegna, Messina, Terbruggen, and in, the 20th century, Eric Gill); Zurbarán painted a saint being crucified upside down.

10

After Giovanni Bellini

One can see Giovanni Bellini's influence in any number of painters. In Vittore Carpaccio, for instance: Carpaccio's *Presentation of Christ in the Temple* is particularly Belliniesque, with its shadowy apse, its cool atmosphere, and the figures placed in quiet, sombre poses. There are even Belliniesque angels sitting below the dais, with the musical instruments. The colouration and tone are Bellini too.

If Bellini's paintings seem subdued compared to many other contemporary painters, the frames around his works add grandeur and glitter. The sublime *Frari Triptych*, for instance, is enclosed in a gorgeous gilt frame. In paintings such as Dosso Dossi and Garofalo's *Ferrara Polyptych* (Pinacoteca Nazionale, Ferrara), the original frame shows how opulent these paintings were. Set amongst flickering candles in darkened interiors of Renaissance churches, these frames would have added a glimmering, incandescent surround to the oil paintings. Bellini works are well-suited to this candlelit interior of so many Italian churches.

One of the amazing things about Giovanni Bellini is his long career, a career which seems to go on as long as his pupil's, Titian. He encompasses so much of Renaissance art, working throughout the 15th century, and two decades into the 16th century. He retained his mastery over the medium to the end, as late works such as *St Jerome and Saints* (S. Giovanni Crisostomo, Venice) show. 'The whole work', writes Jacob Burckhardt, 'shows Bellini still at the height of his powers' (104). In *St Jerome and Saints*, there is much powerful painting, not least in the confident architectural scheme. Bellini orchestrates his large upright figures either side of an archway seen from below. The architectural space is enclosed but soon opens out onto rocks, upon which sits the saint. The wilderness traditionally associated with St Jerome is here brought into the church. The painting acts as a window on the wilderness of St Jerome. The arch acts as a gateway to the wilderness. It is as if a hole has been blown open in the church of S. Giovanni Crisostomo. But, as in all of Bellini's work, this opening is not made by some violent act, by a terrorist bomb, but is an elegant, meticulously crafted arch. It is intended as a gateway to the sublime, as a doorway to calm, pious contemplation. For at the centre of this painting is not the Christ child sitting atop the giant St Christopher, but the outcast St Jerome, who is the model of cultivated humanity: he reads from a book.

In *St Jerome and Saints*, as in just about all of Bellini's paintings, all is quiet and calm. Nothing disturbs the eternal tranquillity of the scene. There are no rough intrusions into the meditative calm. There is nothing in Bellini's picture, for instance, of the frenzy and uncertainty of Raphael's *Transfiguration*, where the bodies gesticulate madly. Not for Bellini this exaggerated art of gesture, as in Titian's *L'Assunta* or Fra Bartolomeo's *St Anne Altarpiece* (Marco Museum, Florence).

The art of Tintoretto, Veronese, Rubens, Michelangelo, Raphael and El Greco seems to be out quite a different order to Bellini's quiet, contemplative style. He is so restrained in his painting. He tries to be unobtrusive, to round off all jagged edges. His is an art of softly rounded corners, an art of smooth contours and volumes smoothed over like clay softened in a sculptor's hands.

Bellini's *Baptism of Christ* (S. Corona, Vicenza), so like Piero's famous *Baptism*, is pervaded by a silence of divinity. Figures on the left make shy gestures of wonder, for this is another moment when Christ's divinity is revealed. Yet, like so many of Bellini's paintings, in the *Baptism* what one notices is the warm colouration, the exquisite detail, the simplicity of the design, and that yellowing sky, as of late evening. It is a masterful depiction of the Baptism, but lacks the authority and mystery of Piero's painting.

Bellini's art remains triumphant because of its brilliant harmonizing of the many elements of painting. In his art, the weighty emotions of religion, embodied in the patriarchs and saints of Christianity with their grey beards and solemn looks, are balanced by the lightness of touch, the warm colouring, the capering and sweet sounds of cherubs and angels.

In Bellini's *Frari Altarpiece*, the Mother of God is flanked by four sombre, suitably humble and regal-looking men. Yet, at her feet, two angels, with chubby limbs and cute faces, make music. Sadly, the Virgin does not feel any of the angels' jollity. She remains, like all of Bellini's beautiful Madonnas, the model of melancholy and humility.

Other painters have created melancholy Madonnas, notably Botticelli, Raphael, Franciabigio, Angelico and Massys, but Bellini's Madonna remains one of the most memorable in the Renaissance.

Notes

1. Dürer, letter to Wilibard Pirckheimer, 7 February 1506, Venice, quoted in R. Goldwater, 78.

2. Rona Goffen: *Giovanni Bellini*, 1. Quotes are from this book unless otherwise stated.

3. P. Gauguin: "Notes Synthetiques", in *Paul Gauguin: A Sketchbook*, tr Raymond Cogniat, Hammer Galleries, New York 1962, 57f.

4. R.M. Rilke: *Tagebücher aus der Frühzeit*, ed Ernst Zinn, Frankfurt, 1973, 21-23; Donald Prater: *A Ringing Glass: The Life of Rainer Maria Rilke*, Clarendon Press 1994, 32, 45.

5. Maurice Denis: "Definition of neotraditionism", 1890, in *Théories: 1890-1910*, Rouart et Watelin, Paris 1920.

6. Jeronimo (Girolamo) Hollivier q. Barthesaris, 29 June 1524, quoted in Rona Goffen, 302.

7. C. G. Jung: *Psychology and Religion: West and East*, Routledge & Kegan Paul 1971, 71.

8. See Erich Neumann, 224.

9. See Philip Hendy: *Piero della Francesca and the Early Renaissance*, London 1968, 17.

10. Bruce Cole, 64f; M. Baxandall: *Painting and Experience*, 11; B.D. Harvey: *Artists' Pigments c. 1600-1835: A Study in English Documentary Sources*, Butterworth Scientific 1982, 47.

11. Plato: *Timeus and Critias*, tr Desmond Lee, Penguin 1977, 69.

12. Julia Kristeva: *The Kristeva Reader*, 262.

13. Julia Kristeva: *The Kristeva Reader*, 247.

14. Julia Kristeva: "Motherhood According to Bellini", *Peinture*, December 1975, no 10-11, and in *The Kristeva Reader*, 243. Page numbers refer to this edition.

15. Chris Mihill, "Breast-feeding falls foul of men", *The Guardian*, Nov 6, 1993.

16. In ib., 237.

17. Andrea Dworkin continues: 'Her nature is different – this time better but still absolutely different – and therefore her role must be different. The worshipping attitude, the spiritual elevation of women that men invoke whenever

they suggest that women are finer than they, proposes that women are what men can never be: chaste, good. In fact men are what women can never be: real moral agents, the bearers of real moral authority and responsibility. Women are not kept from this moral agency by biology, but by a male social system that puts women above or below simple human choice in morally demanding situations. The spiritual superiority of women in this model of ludicrous homage isolates women from the human acts that create meaning, the human choices that create both ethics and history. It separates women out from the chaos and triumph of human responsibility by giving women a two-dimensional morality, a stagnant morality, one in which what is right and good is predetermined, sex-determined, biologically determined.' (Andrea Dworkin: *Right-Wing Women: The Politics of Domesticated Females*, Women's Press 1983, 206.)

18. Julia Kristeva, *Desire in Language*, 246.

19. Julia Kristeva: "Extraterrestrials Suffering For Want of Love", in *Tales of Love*, 374.

20. M. Levey: *Early Renaissance*, 201.

Bibliography

On Giovanni Bellini

Hans Belting. *Giovanni Bellini Pietà: Ikone und Bilderzählung in der venezianischen Malerei*, Frankfurt 1985

Stefano Bottari: *Tutta la pittura di Giovanni Bellini*, Milan 1963

Peter Cannon-Brookes: *The Cornbury Park Bellini: A Contribution towards the Study of the Late Painting of Giovanni Bellini*, Birmingham 1977

David Cast: "The Stork and the Serpent: A New Interpretation of the *Madonna of the Meadow* by Bellini", *Art Quarterly*, 32, 1969, 247-258

Susan J. Delaney: "The iconography of Giovanni Bellini's *Sacred Allegory*", *Art Bulletin*, 59, 1977, 331-5

Colin Eisler: "'Saints Anthony Abbot and Bernardino of Siena'" Designed by Jacopo and Painted by Gentile Bellini", *Arte Veneta*, 39, 1985, 32-40

Everett: "'Coronation of the Virgin'", *Art Bulletin*, 46, 1964, 216-8

J. Fletcher: "Isabella d'Este and Giovanni Bellini's 'Presepio'", *Burlington Magazine*, 123, 1981, 453-67, 602-8

Roger Fry: *Giovanni Bellini*, London 1899

Rona Goffen: *Giovanni Bellini*, Yale University Press, New Haven 1989

—. *Renaissance Venice*, Yale University Press, New Haven 1986

—"Icon and Vision: Giovanni Bellini's Half-Length Madonnas", *Art Bulletin*, 57, 1975, 487-518

—"Giovanni Bellini and the Altarpiece of St. Vincent Ferrer", *Renaissance Studies in Honour of Craig Hugh Smyth*, ed. A. Morrogh, Florence, 1985

Christiane Joost-Gaugier: "A Pair of Miniatures by a Panel Painter: The Earliest Works of Giovanni Bellini?", *Paragone*, 30, 1979, 48-71

Julia Helen Keydel: "A Group of Altarpieces by Giovanni Bellini Considered in Relation to the Context for Which They Were Made", Ph.D thesis, Harvard University 1969

Rodolfa Pallucchini: *Giovanni Bellini*, Milan 1959

Giles Robertson: "The Earlier Works of Giovanni Bellini", *Journal of the Warburg and Courtauld Institutes*, 23, 1960, 45-5

—. *Giovani Bellini*, Oxford, 1968

Martin Robertson: "A Possible Classical Echo in Bellini", *Burlington Magazine*, 121, 1979, 650-3

Carolyn Wilson: "Giovanni Bellini's *Pesaro Altarpiece*, Studies in Its Context and Meaning", Ph.D thesis, Institute of Fine Arts, 1976

Edgar Wind: *Bellini's Feast of the Gods: A Study of Venetian Humanism*, Cambridge, Mass., 1948

Others

Emile de Antonio & Mitch Tuchman: *Painters Painting*, Abbeville Press, New York 1984

C.G. Argan: *The Renaissance*, Thames & Hudson 1969

Karen Armstrong: *The Gospel According to Woman; Christianity's Creation of the Sex War in the West*, Pan 1987

Geoffrey Ashe: *The Virgin: Mary's Cult and the Re-emergence of the Goddess*, Arkana 1987

Patrick Bade: *Femme Fatale: Images of evil and fascinating women*, Ash & Grant 1979

Michael Baxandall: *Painting and Experience in 15th Century Italy*, Oxford University Press 1988

—*Patterns of Intention: On the Historical Explanation of Pictures*, Yale University Press 1985

James Beck: *Italian Renaissance Painting*, Harper & Row, New York 1981

Ean Begg: *The Cult of the Black Virgin*, Routledge 1985

Bernard Berenson: *The Italian Painters of the Renaissance*, Phaidon 1952

—*Looking at Pictures with Bernard Berenson*, selected by Hann Kiel, Abrahams, New York 1974

Pamela Berger: *The Goddess Obscured*, Robert Hale 1988

Bruce Bernard: *The Queen of Heaven: A Selection of Painting the Virgin from the Twelfth to the Eighteenth Centuries*, Macdonald/ Orbis 1987

—*The Bible and Its Painters*, Orbis 1983

Carlo Bertelli: *Piero della Francesca*, Yale University Press, New Haven 1992

Anthony Bertram: *Piero della Francesca*, Studio Publications 1949

Frances Bonner, *et al*, eds: *Imagining Women Cultural Representations and Gender*, Polity Press, Cambridge 1992

Botticelli: *The Complete Paintings of Botticelli*, Granada 1980

Serge Bramly: *Leonardo: The Artist and the Man*, Michael Joseph 1992

Allan Brahama: *Italian Renaissance Painters of the Sixteenth Century*, National Gallery 1985

Robert Briffault: *The Mothers: A Study of the origins of Sentiments and Institutions*, Allen & Unwin, 3 vols 1927

Stephanie Brown: *Religious Painting*, Phaidon 1979

Jacob Burckhardt: *The Altarpiece in Renaissance Italy*, Phaidon 1988

Titus Burckhardt: *Sacred Art in East and West*, Perennial Book, Middlesex 1967

Ritchie Calder: *Leonardo and The Age of the Eye*, Heinemann 1970

Joseph Campbell: *The Power of Myth*, with Bill Moyers, ed. Betty Sue Flowers, Doubleday, New York 1988

Michael P. Carroll: *The Cult of the Virgin Mary*, Princeton University Press, New Jersey 1986

Whitney Chadwick: *Women, Art, and Society*, Thames & Hudson 1990

Andre Chastel: *Art of the Italian Renaissance*, tr Peter & Linda Murray, Alpine Fine Arts Collection 1985

—*The Studios and Styles of the Renaissance, Italy 1460-1500*, tr Griffin, Thames & Hudson 1966

Herschel B. Chipp, ed. *Theories of Modern Art*, University Press of California, Los Angeles 1968

J.E. Cirlot: *A Dictionary of Symbols*, Routledge 1981

Kenneth Clark: *Landscape into Art*, Reader's Union 1965

—*Piero della Francesca*, Phaidon 1969

Bruce Cole: *The Renaissance Artist at Work*, John Murray 1983

—*Piero della Francesca: Tradition and Innovation in Renaissance Art, Harper ancesca: Tradition and Innovation in Renaissance Art*, Harper n S. Roudiez, Columbia University Press 1987

J.C. Cooper: *An Illustrated Dictionary of Traditional Symbols*, Thames & Hudson 1978

Pierre Courthion: *Flemish Painting*, Thames & Hudson 1958

Martin Davies: *Rogier van der Weyden*, Phaidon 1972

Lene Dresen-Coenders, ed: *Saints and She-Devils: Images of Women in the 15th and 16th Centuries*, Rubicon Press 1987

Georges Duby & Michele Perrot: *Power and Beauty: Images of Women in Art*, Tauris Parke Books,

Andrea Dworkin: *Intercourse*, Arrow 1988

—*Pornography: Men Possessing Women*, Women's Press 1984

Colin Eisler: *Early Netherlandish Painting: The Thyssen-Bornemisza Collection*, Sotheby's Publications 1989

Mircea Eliade: *Ordeal by Labyrinth*, University of Chicago Press 1984

—*A History of Religious Ideas, I*, Collins 1979

—*Patterns in Comparative Religion*, Sheed & Ward 1958

—*Symbolism, the Sacred and the Arts*, Crossroad, New York 1985

Joan Evans, ed: *The Flowering of the Middle Ages*, Thames & Hudson 1966

Giorgio T. Faggin: *The Complete Paintings of the Van Eycks*, Weidenfeld & Nicolson 1970

George Ferguson: *Signs and Symbols in Christian Art*, Oxford University Press 1961

John Ferguson: *An Illustrated Encyclopaedia of Mysticism*, Thames & Hudson 1976

Peter Fingesten: *The Eclipse of Symbolism*, University Press of California 1970

S.J. Freedberg: *Painting of the High Renaissance in Rome and Florence*, Harper & Row, New York 1972

Sigmund Freud: *Leonardo da Vinci*, tr Alan Tyson, Penguin 1963

Max J. Friedlander: *From Van Eyck to Bruegel*, Phaidon 1969

Elinor Gadon: *The Once and Future Goddess*, Aquarian Press 1990

Niny Garavaghlia: *The Complete Paintings of Mantegna*, Weidenfeld & Nicholson 1971

Fred Gettings: *The Hidden Art: A Study of the Occult Symbolism in Art*, Studio Vista 1978

Marija Gimbutas: *The Language of the Goddess*, Thames & Hudson 1989

Carlo Ginzburg: *The Enigma of Piero: Piero della Francesca, The Baptism, The Arezzo Cycle, The Flagellation*, Verso 1985

Rona Goffen: *Giovanni Bellini*, Yale University Press, New Haven 1989

Robert Goldwater & Marco Treves, eds. *Artists on Art*, John Murray 1975

E.H. Gombrich. *Symbolic Images*, Phaidon, 1985

—. *Norm and Form*, Phaidon, 1985

Cecil Gould: *Leonardo: The Artist and the Non-Artist*, Weidenfeld & Nicholson 1975

John Hale: *Italian Renaissance Painting*, Phaidon 1977

F.C.Happold, ed. *Mysticism*, Penguin 1970

Frederick Hartt: *History of Italian Renaissance Art: Painting, Sculpture, Architecture*, Thomas & Hudson 1987

—*Sandro Botticelli*, Collins 1954

Michael Jacobs: *A Guide to European Painting*, David & Charles 1980

Diane Kelder: *Pageant of the Renaissance*, Pall Mall Press 1969

Julia Kristeva. *The Kristeva Reader*, ed. Toril Moi, Blackwell, Oxford, 1986

—. *Desire in Language: A Semiotic Approach to Literature and Art*, ed. Leon Roudiez, tr. Thomas Gora, Alice Jardine & Leon Roudiez, Blackwell, Oxford, 1982

—. *Black Sun: Depression and Melancholy*, tr. L.S. Roudiez, Columbia University Press, New York, NY, 1989

—. *Strangers to Ourselves*, tr. L.S. Roudiez, Harvester Wheatsheaf, Hemel Hempstead, 1991

—. *About Chinese Women*, tr. A. Barrows, Boyars, 1977

—. *Tales of Love*, tr. Leon S. Roudiez, Columbia University Press, New York, NY, 1987

—. *Revolution in Poetic Language*, tr. Margaret Walker, Columbia University Press, New York, NY, 1984

—. *Powers of Horror: An Essay on Abjection*, tr. Leon S. Roudiez, Columbia University Press, New York, NY, 1982

Weston La Barre: *The Ghost Dance*, Allen & Unwin 1972

Leonardo da Vinci: *The Drawings of Leonarrillan*, New York 1961

—*The Complete Paintings*, introduction by L.D. Ettinger, Weidenfeld & Nicolson 1969

—*Selections from the Notebooks*, Oxford University Press 1952

Michael Levey: *High Renaissance*, Penguin 1975

—*Early Renaissance*, Penguin 1967

Lucy Lippard: *From the Center: feminist essays on women's art*, Dutton, New York 1976

Christopher Lloyd: *Fra Angelico*, Phaidon 1979

—*A Picture History of Art*, Phaidon 1979

Fiona MacCarthy: *Eric Gill*, Faber 1989

Emile Male: *The Gothic Image*, Collins 1961

K.B. MacFarlane: *Hans Memling*, Clarendon Press 1971

Roy McMullen: *Mona Lisa: The Picture and the Myth*, Macmillan 1975

J.C.J. Metford: *Dictionary of Christian Lore and Legend*, Thames & Hudson 1983

Michelangelo: *The Complete Paintings*, Granada 1980

Toril Moi: *Sexual/ Textual Politics: Feminist Literary Theory*, Routledge 1988

Edward Mullins: *The Painted Witch: Female Body, Male Art*, Secker & Warburg 1985

Peter & Linda Murray: *The Penguin Dictionary of Art and Artists*, Penguin 1976

Linda Murray: *High Renaissance*, Thames & Hudson 1977

Lynda Nead: *Female Nude: Art, Obscenity and Sexuality*, Routledge 1992

Erich Neumann: *The Great Mother*, Princeton University Press, New Jersey 1972

Shirley Nicholson, ed. *The Goddess Re-awakening: The Goddess Principle Today*, Theosophical Publishing House, New York 1989

Rudolf Otto: *The Idea of the Holy*, Oxford University Press 1958

Erwin Panofsky: *Studies in Iconology*, Harper & Row, New York 1972

—*Early Netherlandish Painting*, Harvard University Press, Mass., 1953

Rozsika Parker & Griselda Pollock: *Old Mistresses: Women, Art and ideology*, Routledge & Kegan Paul 1981

Geoffrey Parrinder: *Mysticism in the World's Religions*, Sheldon Press 1976

Walter Pater: *The Renaissance*, Oxford University Press 1980

Michael Payne: *Reading Theory: An Introduction to Lacan, Derrida, and Kristeva*, Blackwell 1993

Robert Payne: *Leonardo da Vinci*, Robert Hale 1979

Karen Petersen & J.J. Wilson: *Women Artists: Recognition and Reappraisal from the Early Middle Ages to the Twentieth Century*, Women's Press, 1978

Piero della Francesca: *The Complete Paintings of Piero della Francesca*, intr. Peter Murray, notes by Pierluigi de Vecchi, Penguin, 1985

Griselda Pollock: *Vision and Difference: femininity, feminism and histories of art*, Routledge 1988

John Pope-Hennessy: *Fra Angelico*, Phaidon 1974

Jeremy Robinson: *Glorification: Religious Abstraction in Renaissance and 20th Century Painting*, Crescent Moon 1994

—*The Madonna Glorified: The Paintings of Karen Arthurs and the Exhibition Hours of the Virgin, Based on Scenes From the Life of the Virgin Mary*, Crescent Moon 1991

Robert Rosenblum: *Modern Painting and the Northern Romantic Tradition*, Thames & Hudson 1978

Mark Roskill: *What is Art History?*, Thames & Hudson 1976

John Ruskin: *Works*, ed. E. T.Cook & A.Wedderburn, 39 vols, Allen 1903-12

Monica Sjöö & Barbara Mor: *The Great Cosmic Mother*, Harper & Row, San Francisco 1987

Alistair Smith: *Early Netherlandish and German Painting*, National Gallery 1985

Frank Stella: *Working Space*, Harvard University Press, Cambridge, Mass., 1986

Victor I. Stoichita: *Leonardo da Vinci*, Abbey Library 1978

Susan Rubin Suleiman, ed: *The Female Body in Western Culture: Contemporary Perspectives*, Harvard University Press, Cambridge, Mass., 1986

Nicholas Usherwood: *The Bible in 20th Century Art*, Pagoda Books 1987

Lionello Venturi: *Renaissance Painting, from Leonardo to Dürer*, Skira/ Macmillan 1979

—*Italian Paintings*, Zwemmer 1950

—*Botticelli*, Phaidon 1964

M. Warner. *Alone Of All Her Sex: The Myth and Cult of the Virgin Mary*, Picador

    1985
—*Monuments and Maidens*, Weidenfeld & Nicholson 1985
Alan Watts: *The Myth and Ritual of Christianity*, Thames & Hudson 1983
Margaret Whinney: *Early Flemish Painters*, Faber 1966
John White: *The Birth and Rebirth of Pictorial Space*, Faber 1957/87
Edward C.Whitmont: *Return of the Goddess*, Routledge 1987

Illustrations

Pictures by Giovanni Bellini, followed by some of his contemporaries.

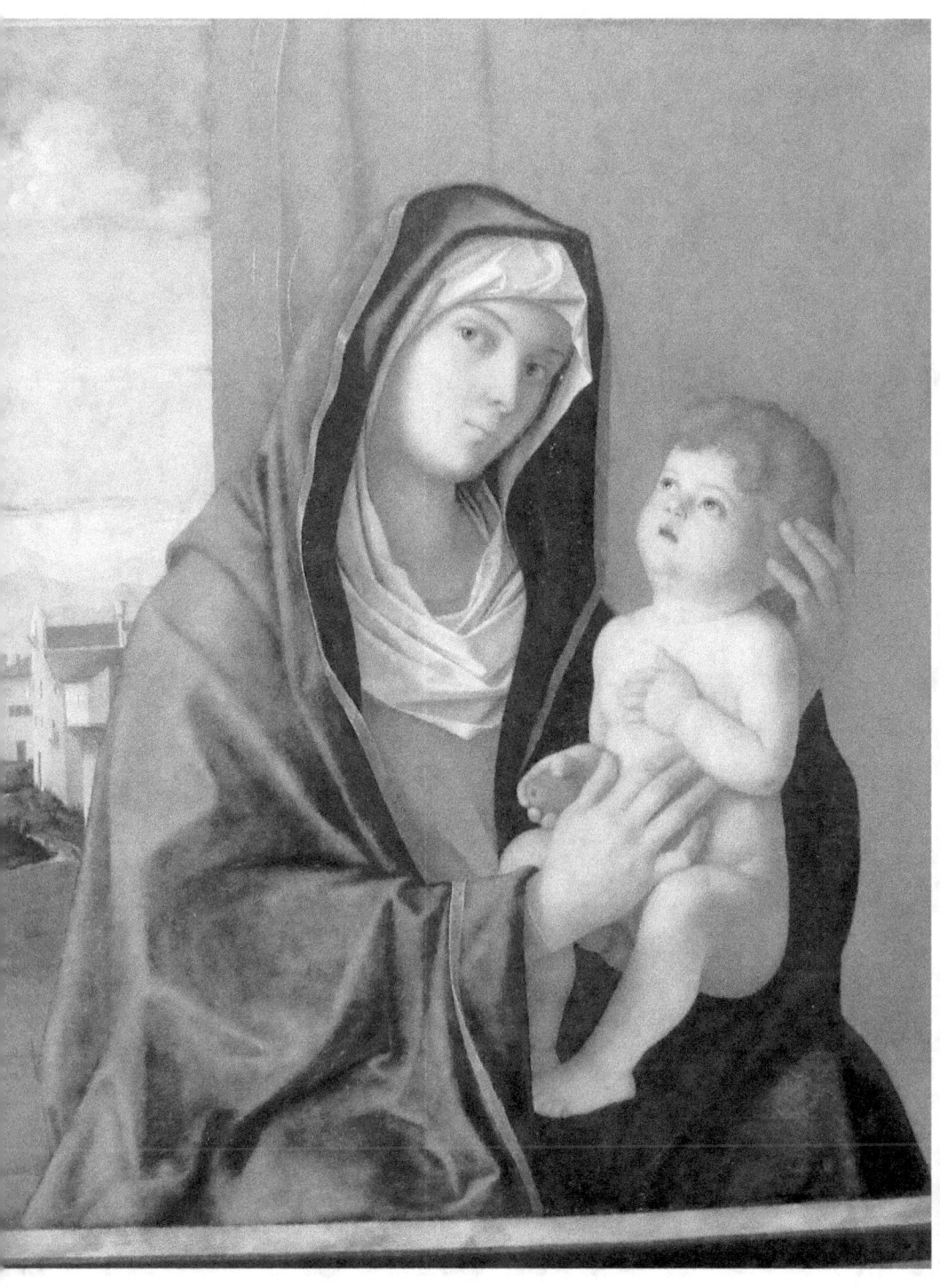

Giovanni Bellini, Virgin and Child, Metropolitan Museum,
New York City

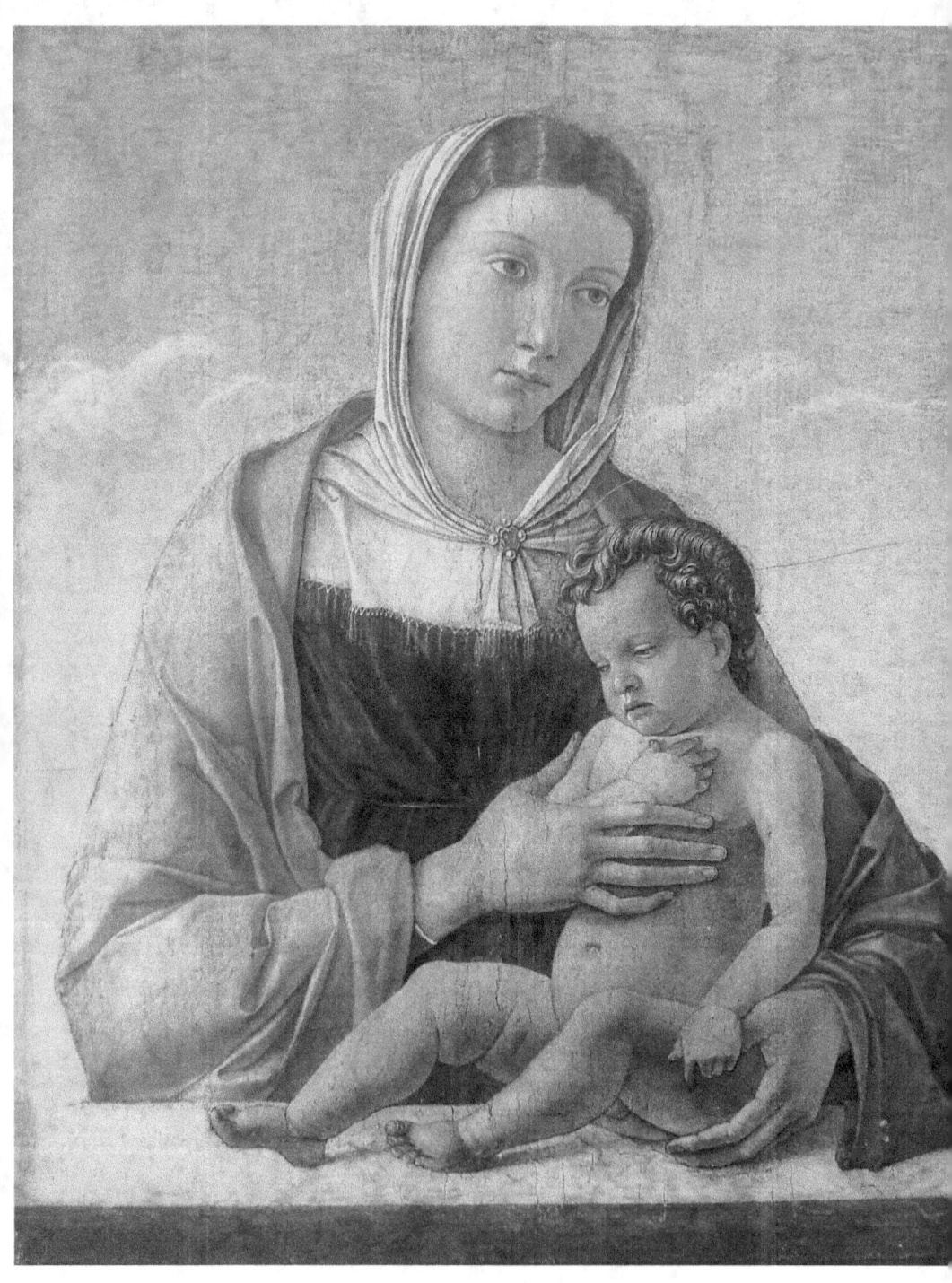

Giovanni Bellini, Madona and Child, Museo Correr e
Quadreria Correr, Venice

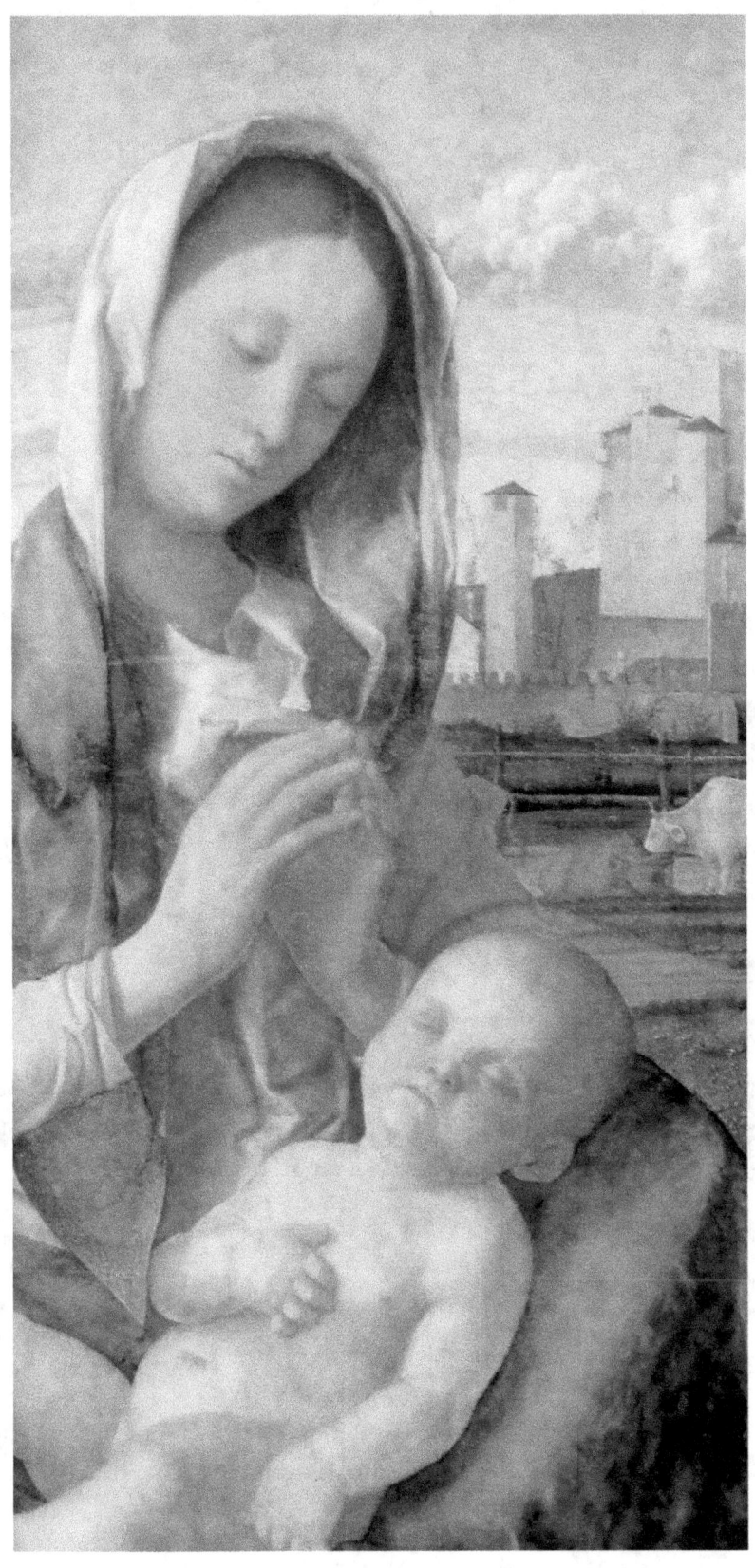

Giovanni Bellini, The Madonna of the Meadow, detail

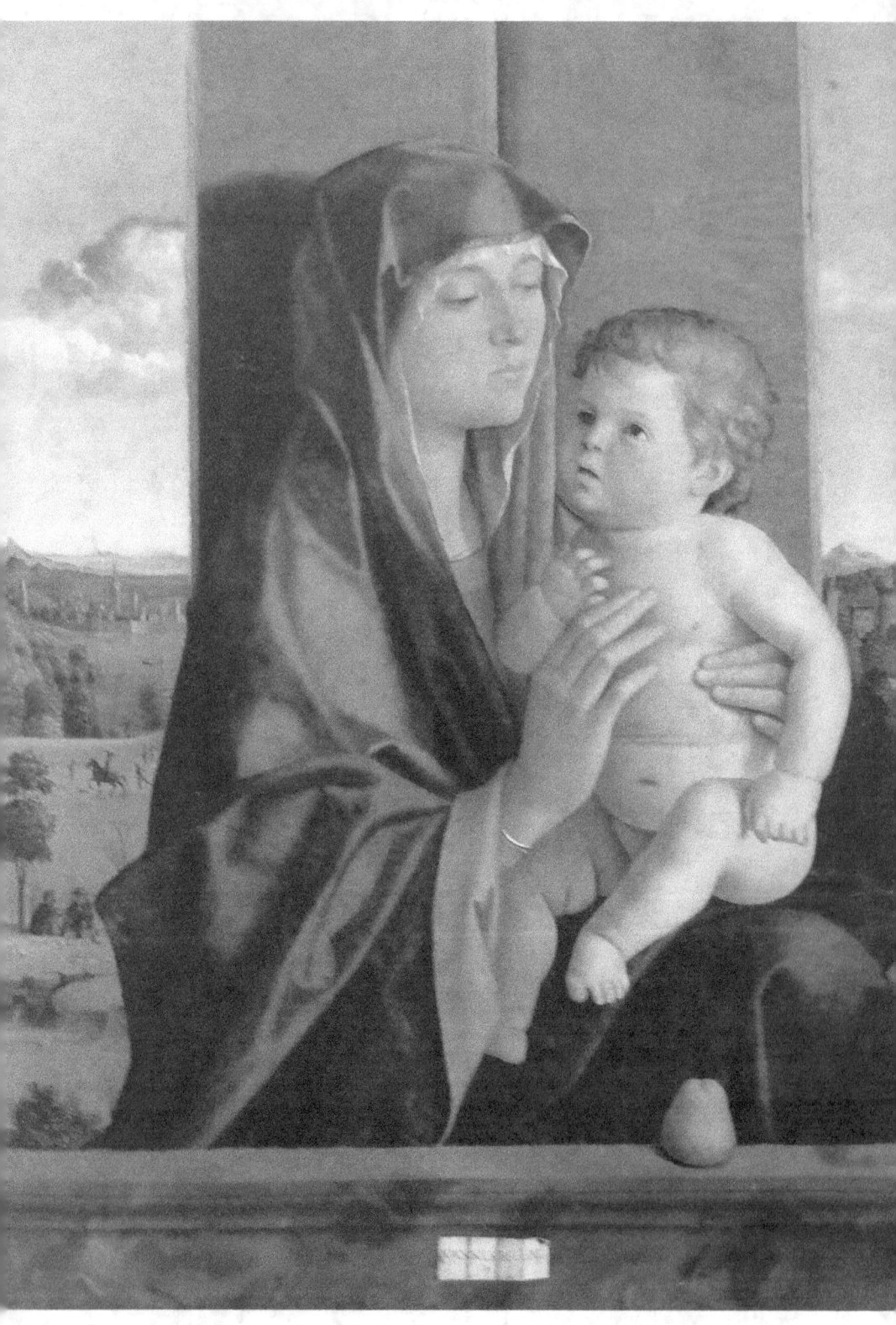

Giovanni Bellini, The Virgin and Child, Bergamo

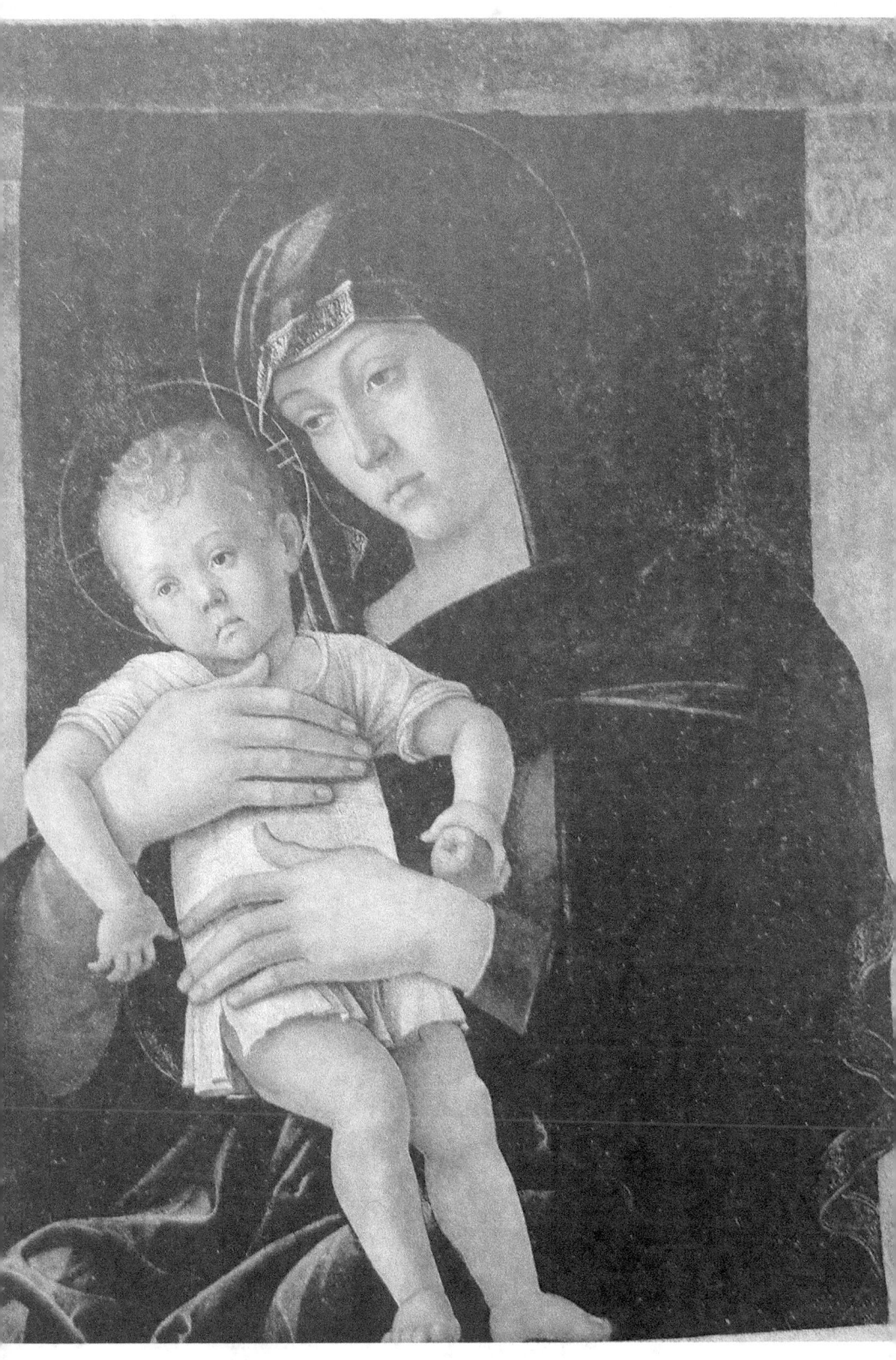

Giovanni Bellini, The Virgin and Child, Pinacoteca de Brera, Milan

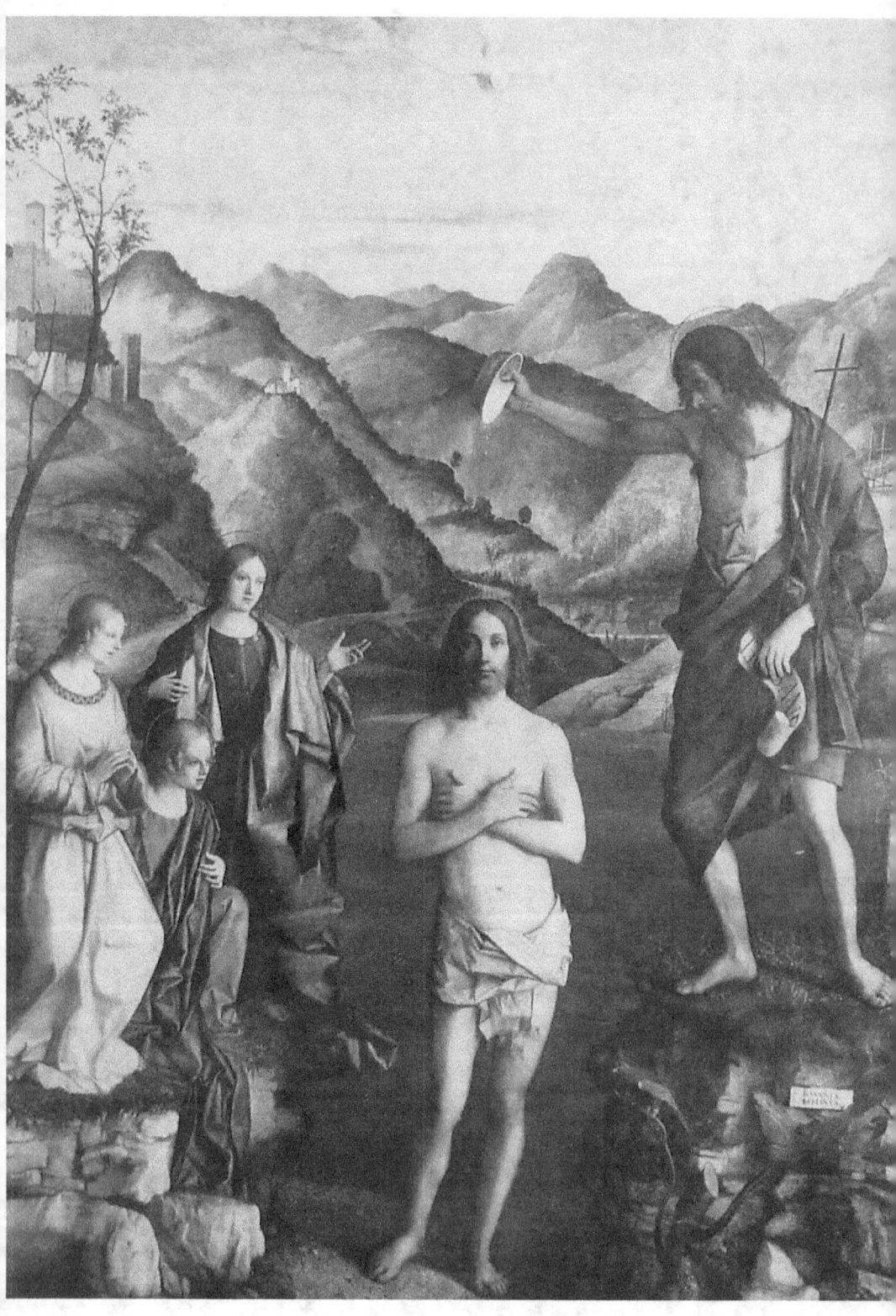

Giovanni Bellini, Baptism, early 16th century

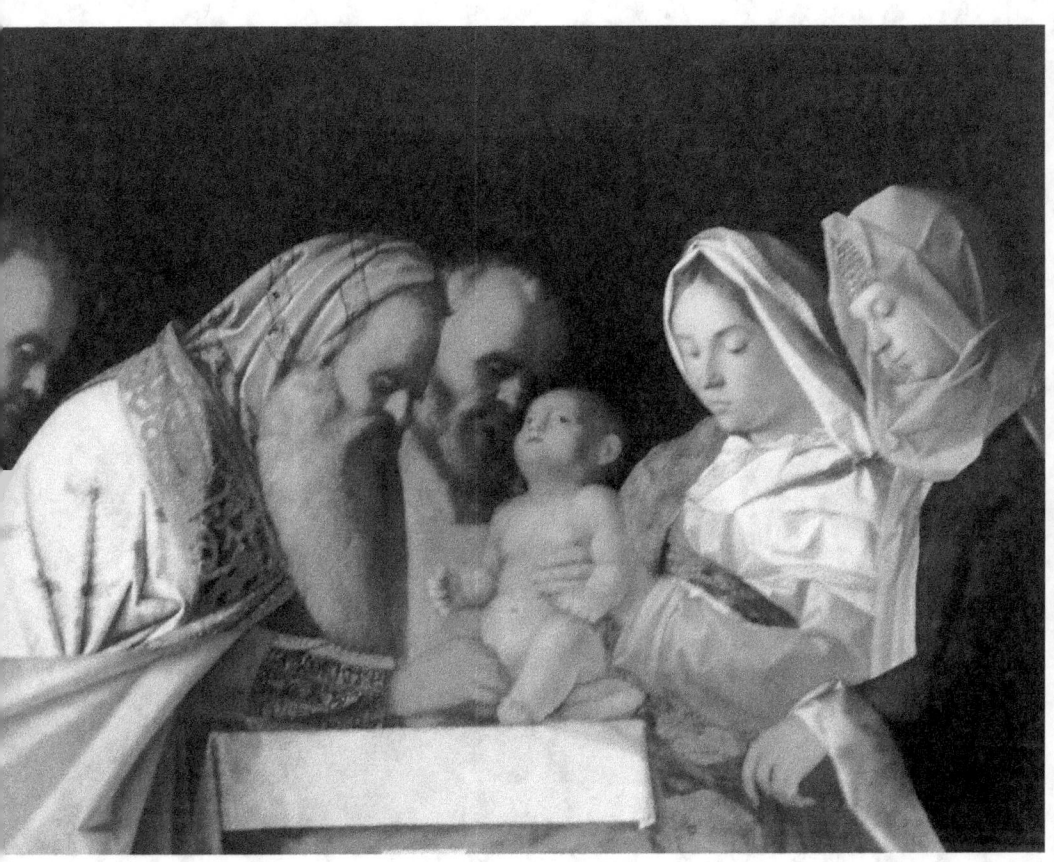

Giovanni Bellini, The Circumcision, National Gallery, London

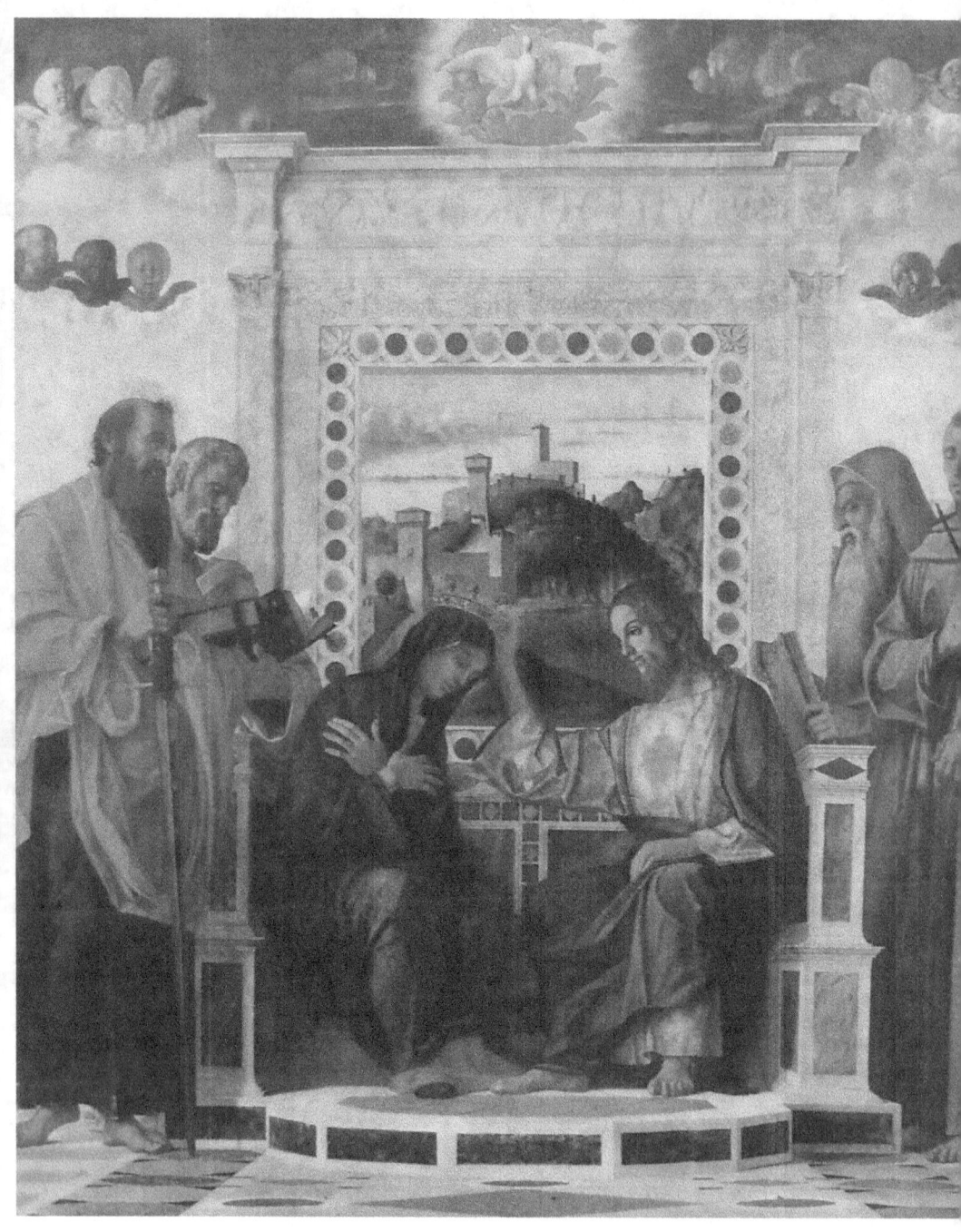

Giovanni Bellini, The Coronation of the Virgin, Pesaro

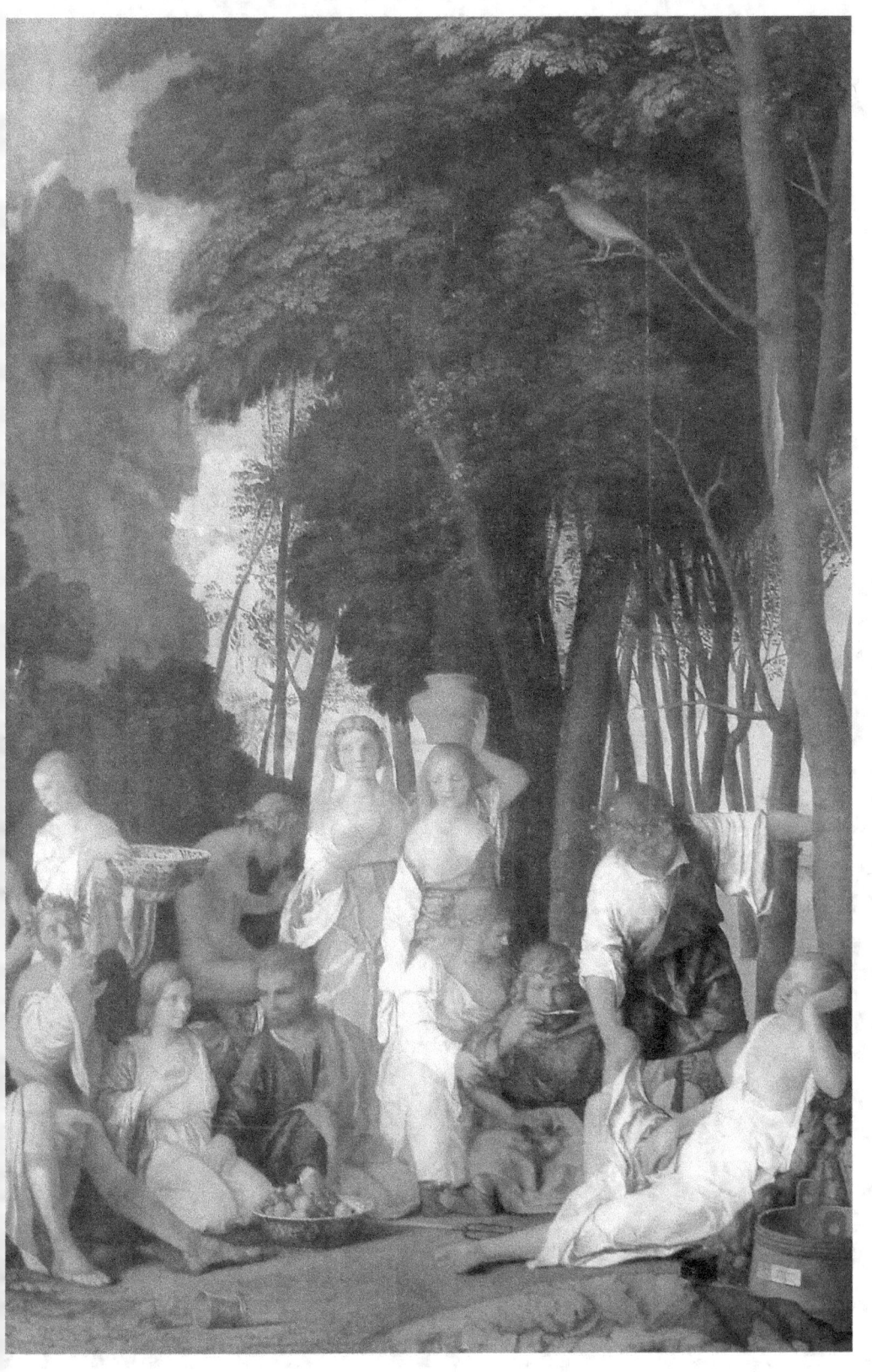

Giovanni Bellini, The Feast of the Gods, 1514, National Gallery of Art, Washington

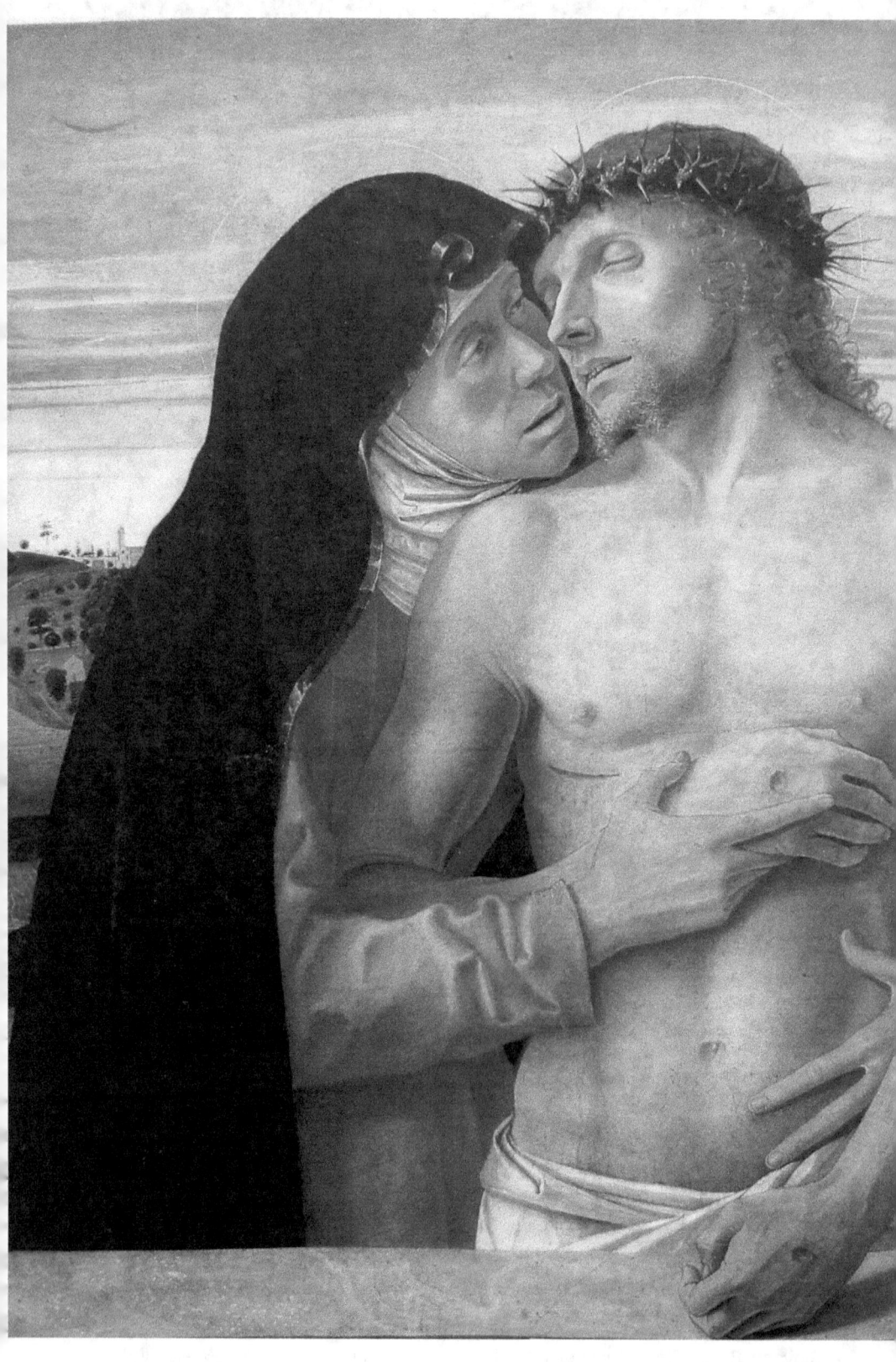

Giovanni Bellini, Pietà, Milan

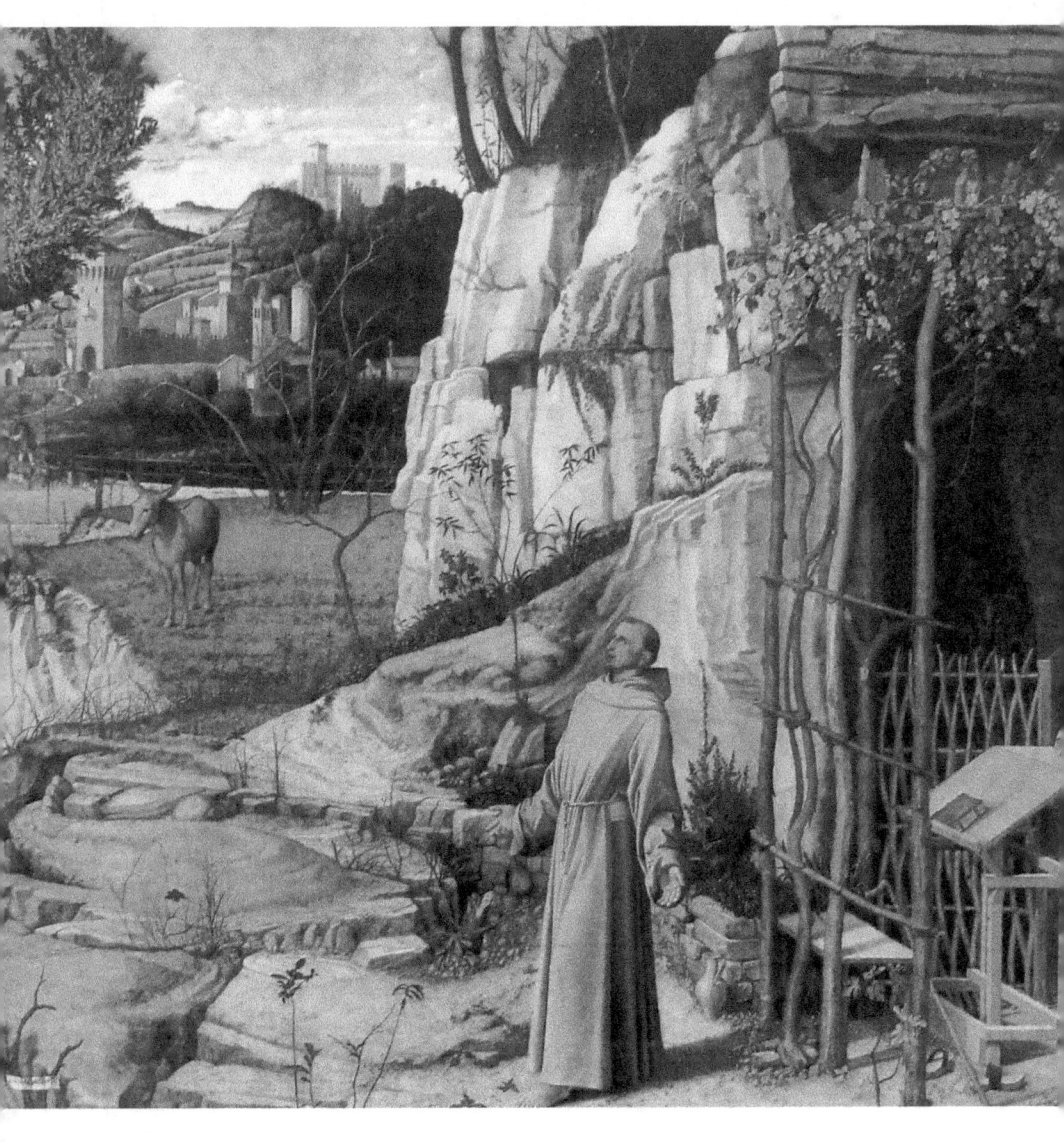

Giovanni Bellini, The Ecstasy of St Francis, Frick Collection, New York

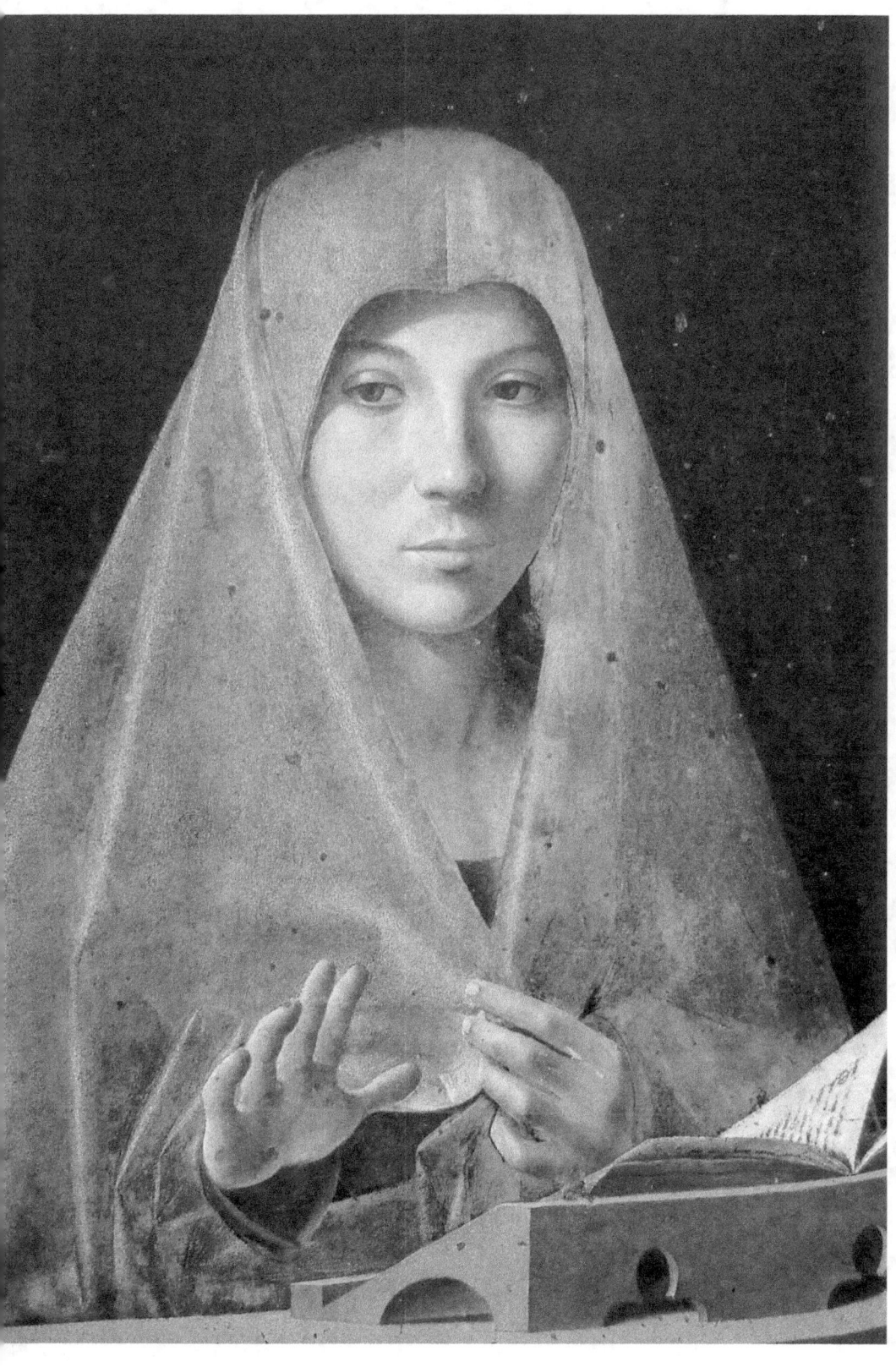

Antonello da Messina, The Virgin of the Annunciation, 1475, Palermo

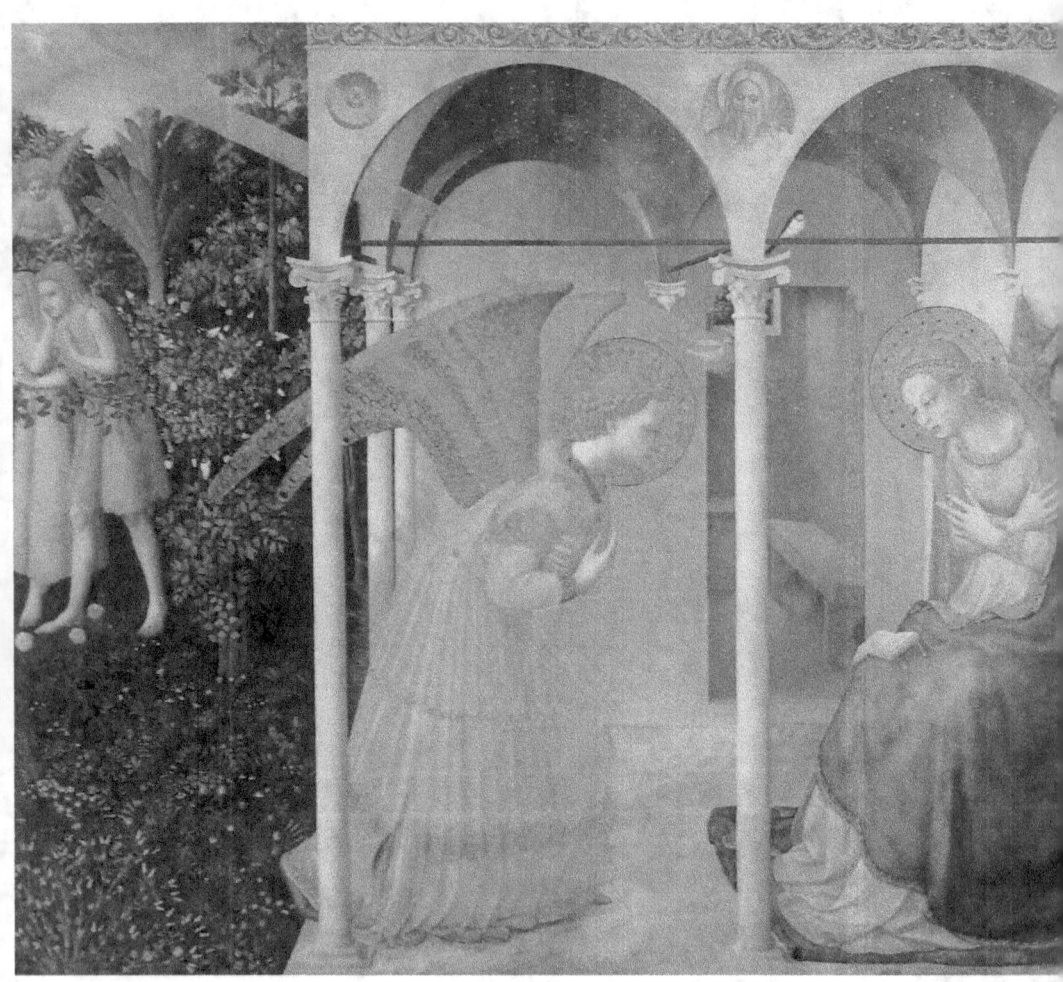

Fra Angelico, Annunciation, Prado, Madrid

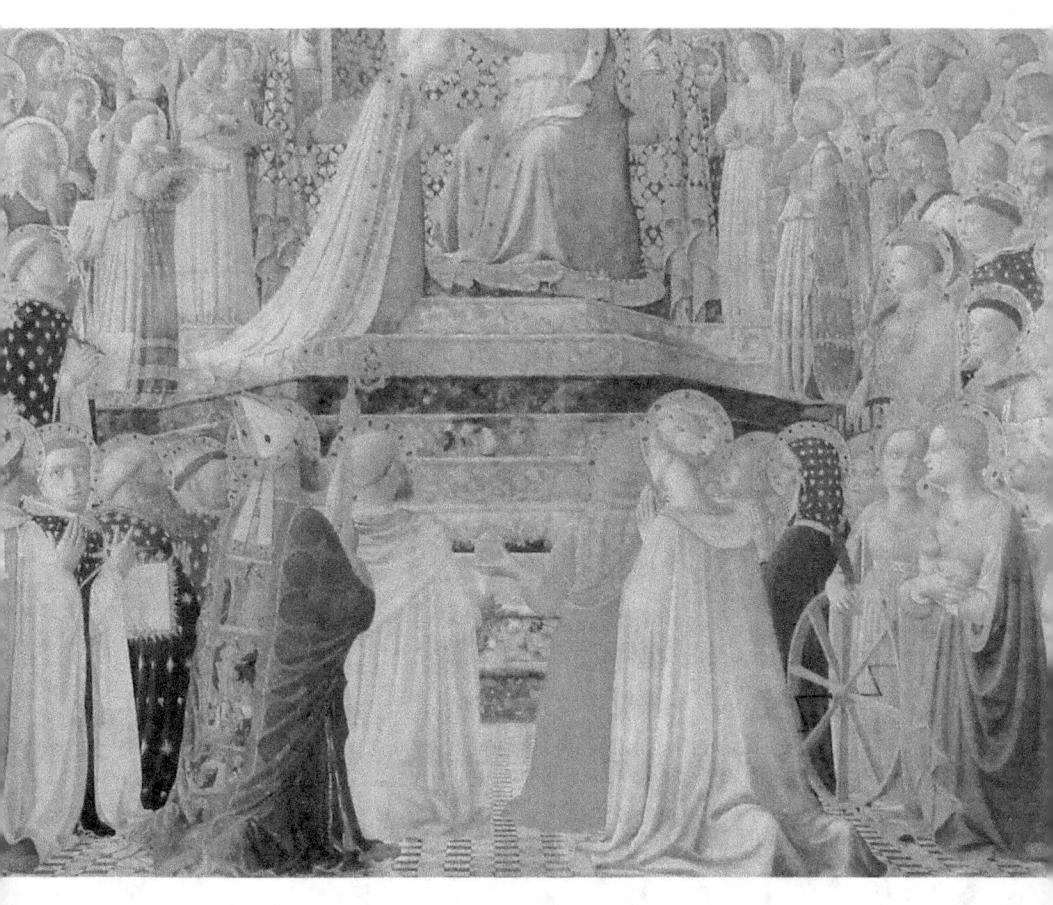

Fra Angelico, The Coronation of the Virgin, Louve, Paris, detail

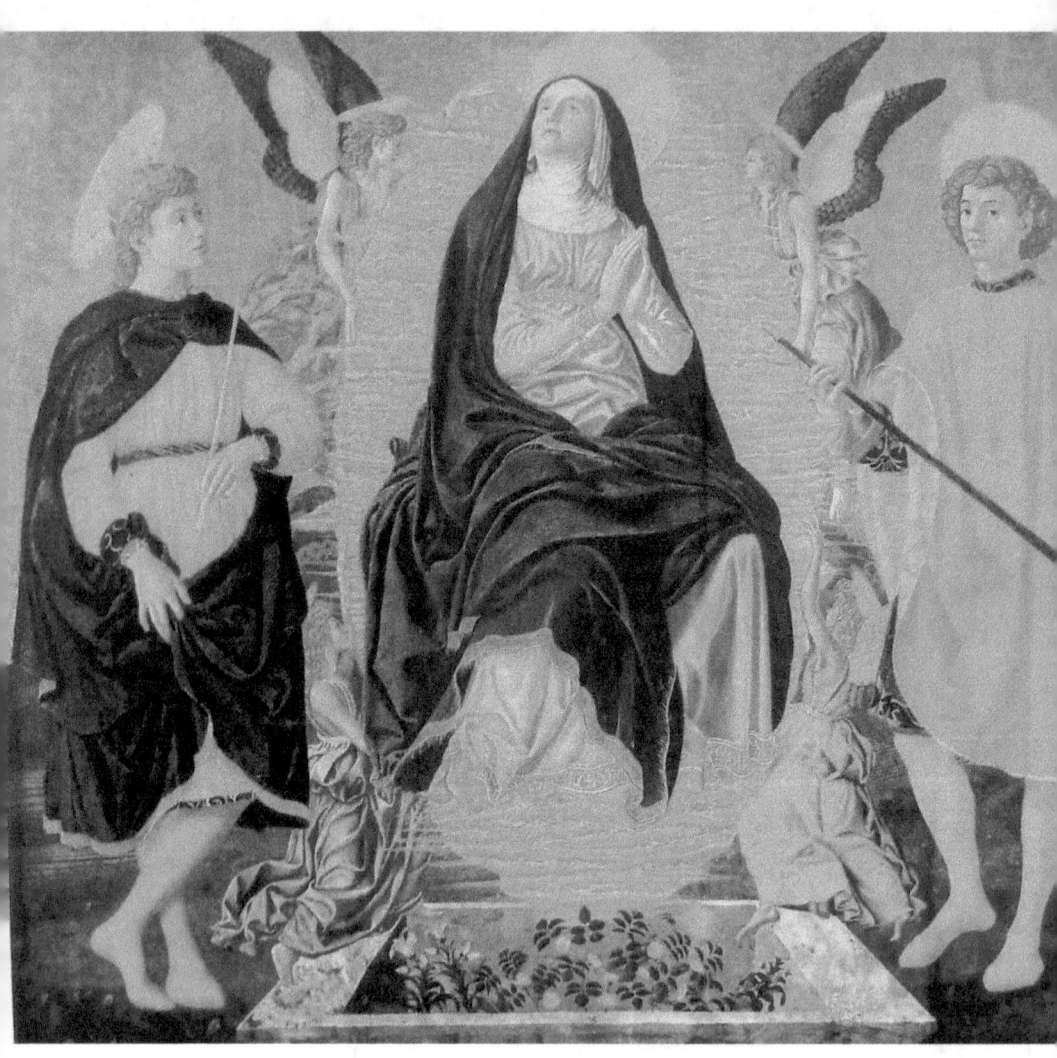

Andrea del Castagno, Assumption, Berlin

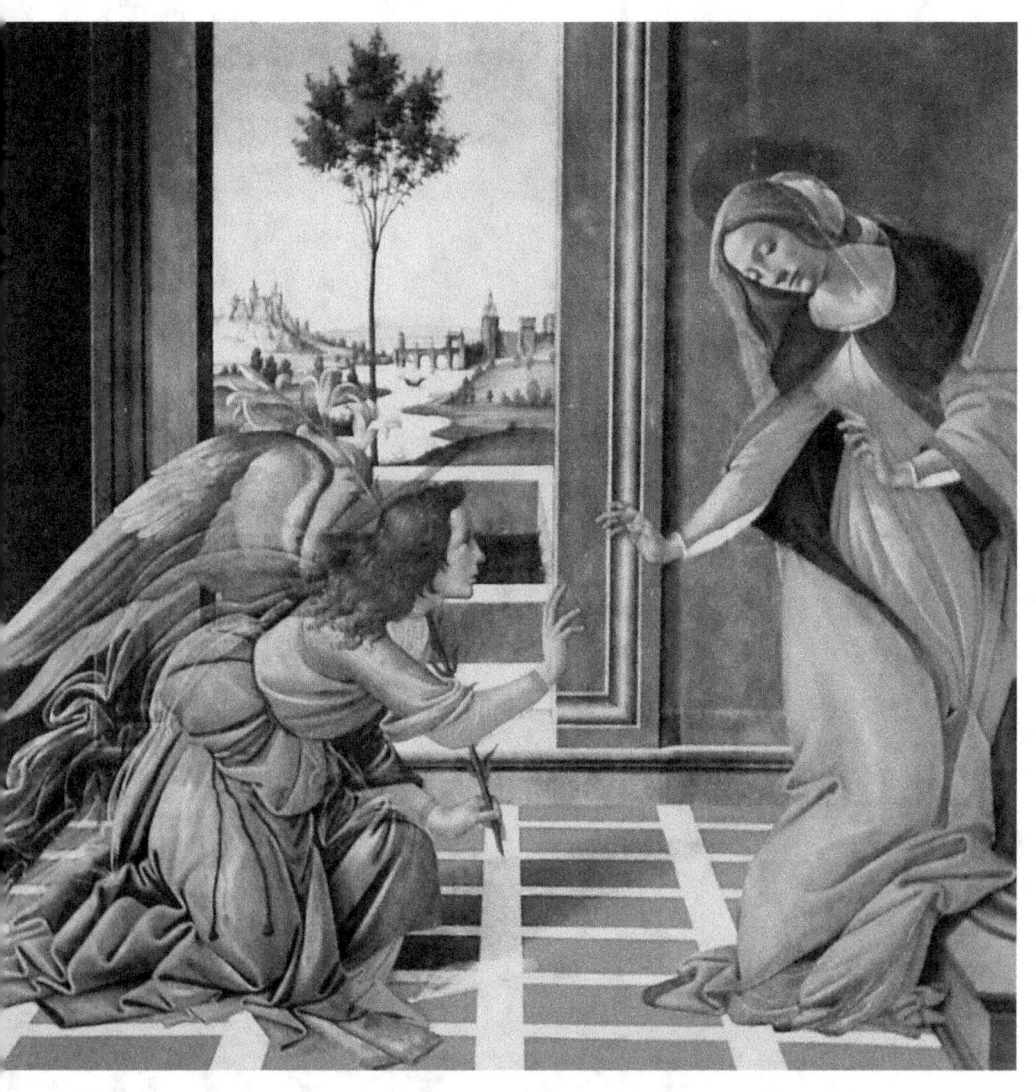

Sandro Botticelli, The Annunciation, Uffizi Gallery, Florence

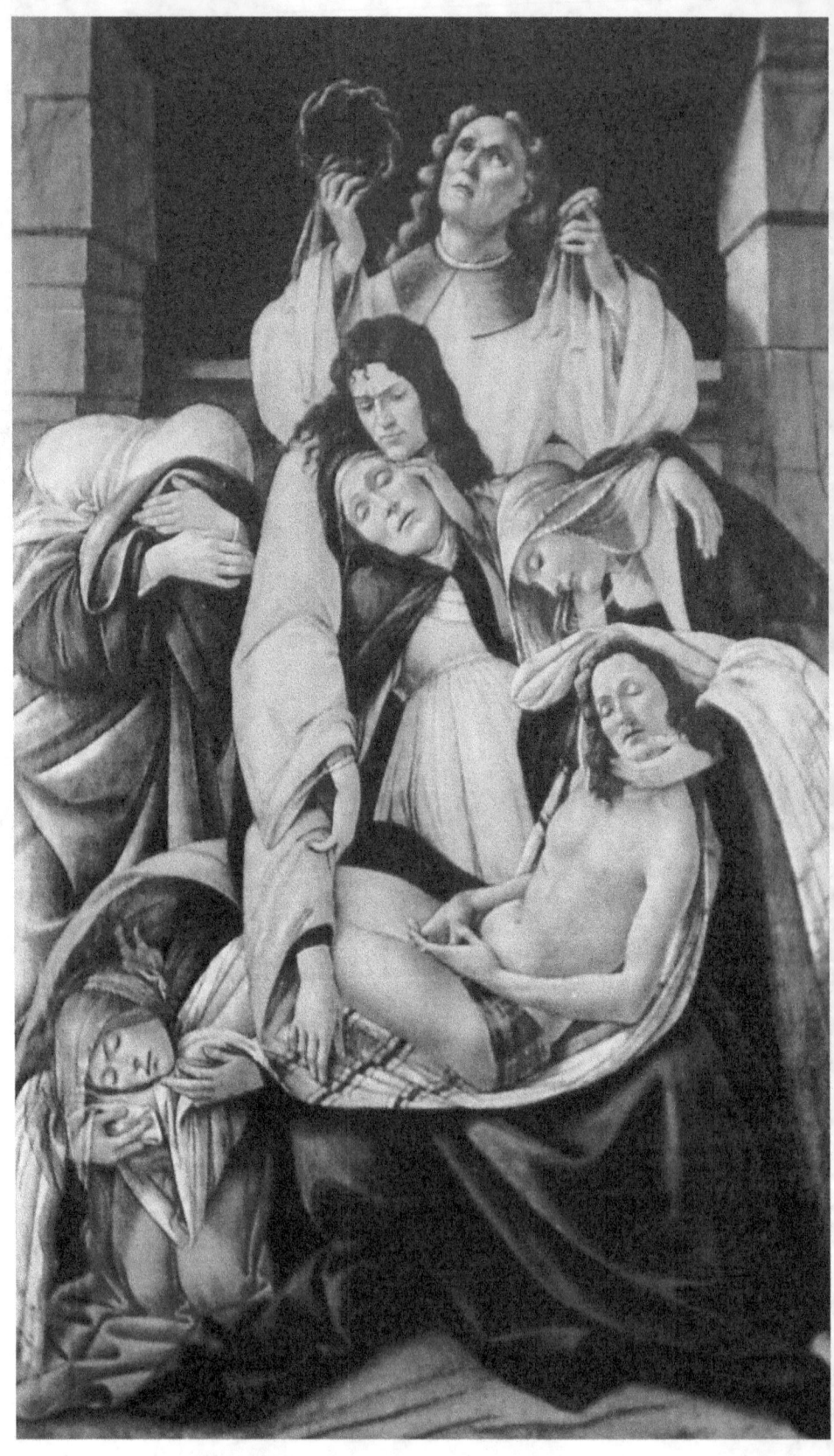

Sandro Botticelli, Pietà, Milan

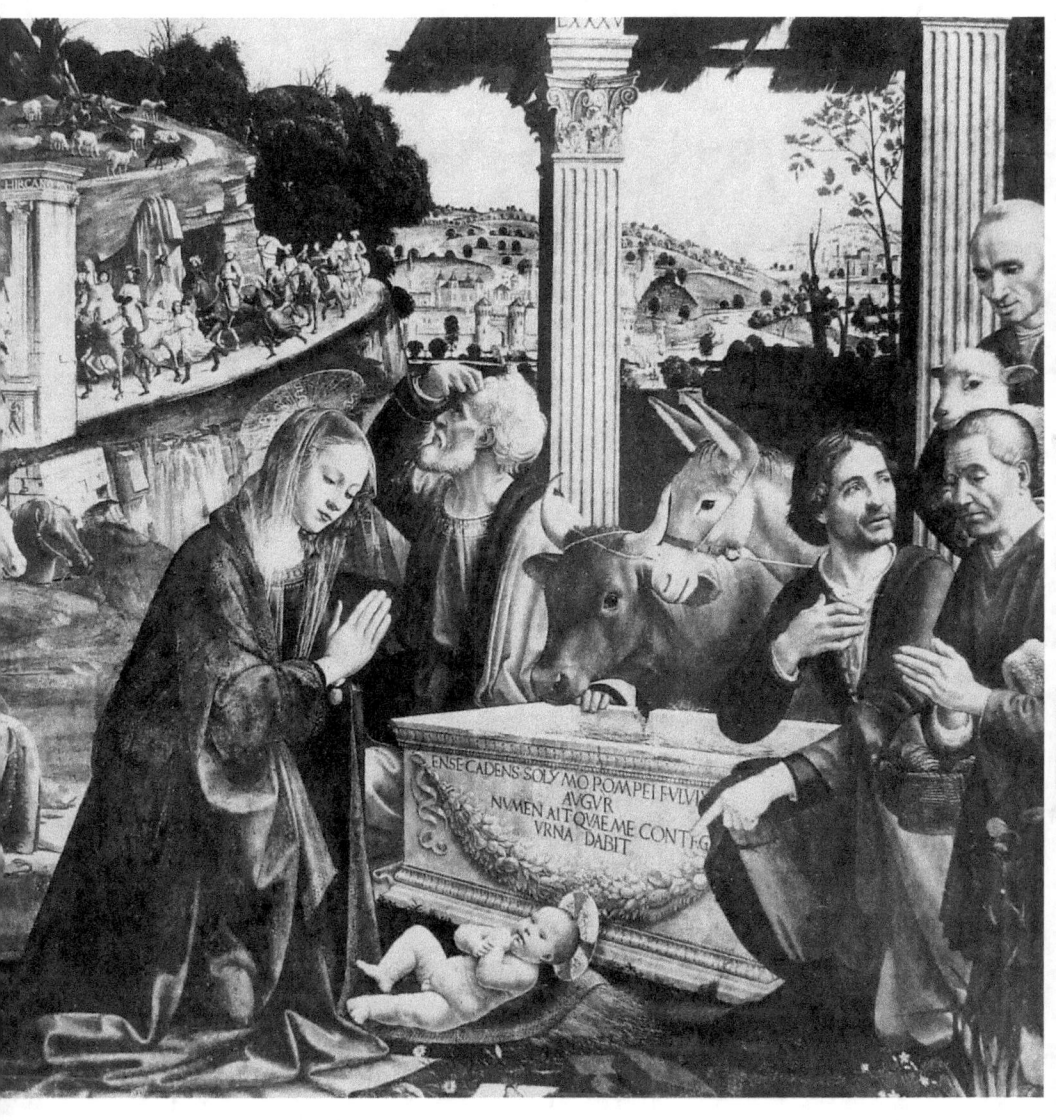

Domenico Ghirlandaio, Adoration of the Shepherds, 1485

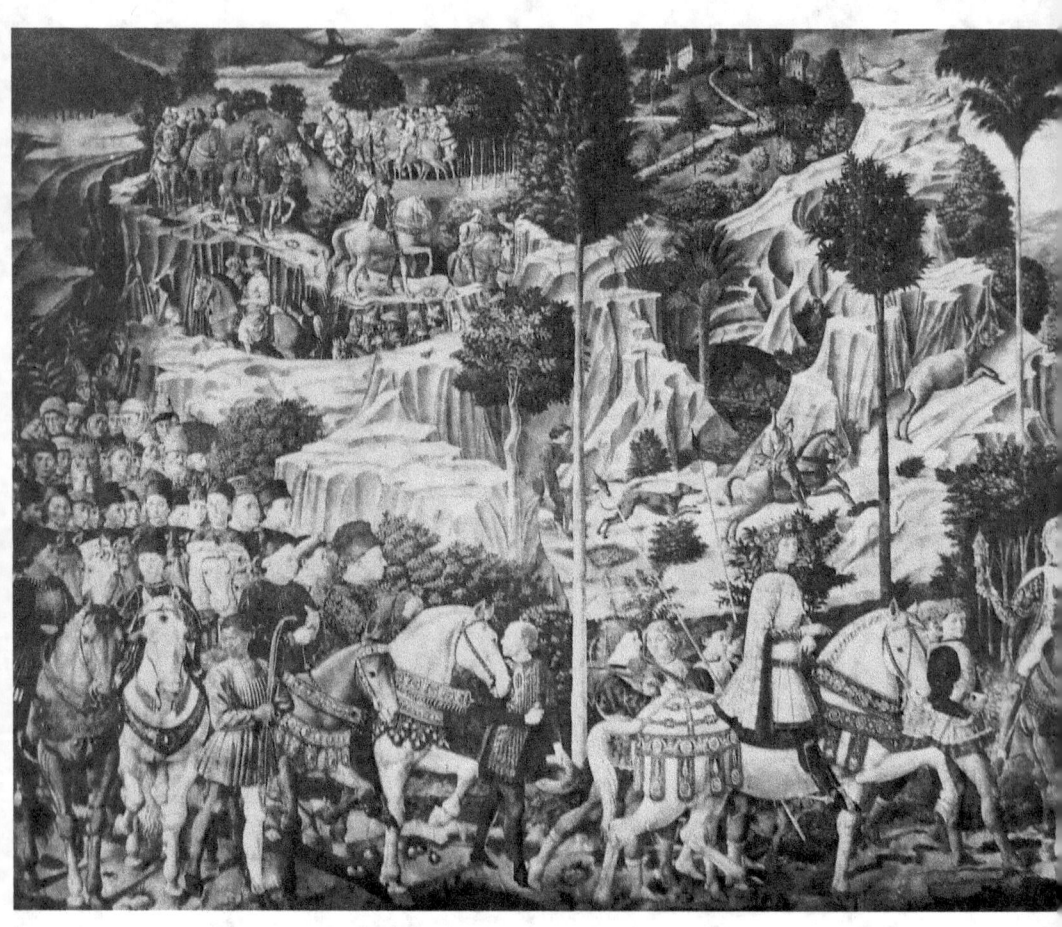

Benozzo Gozzoli, *Journey of the Magi*

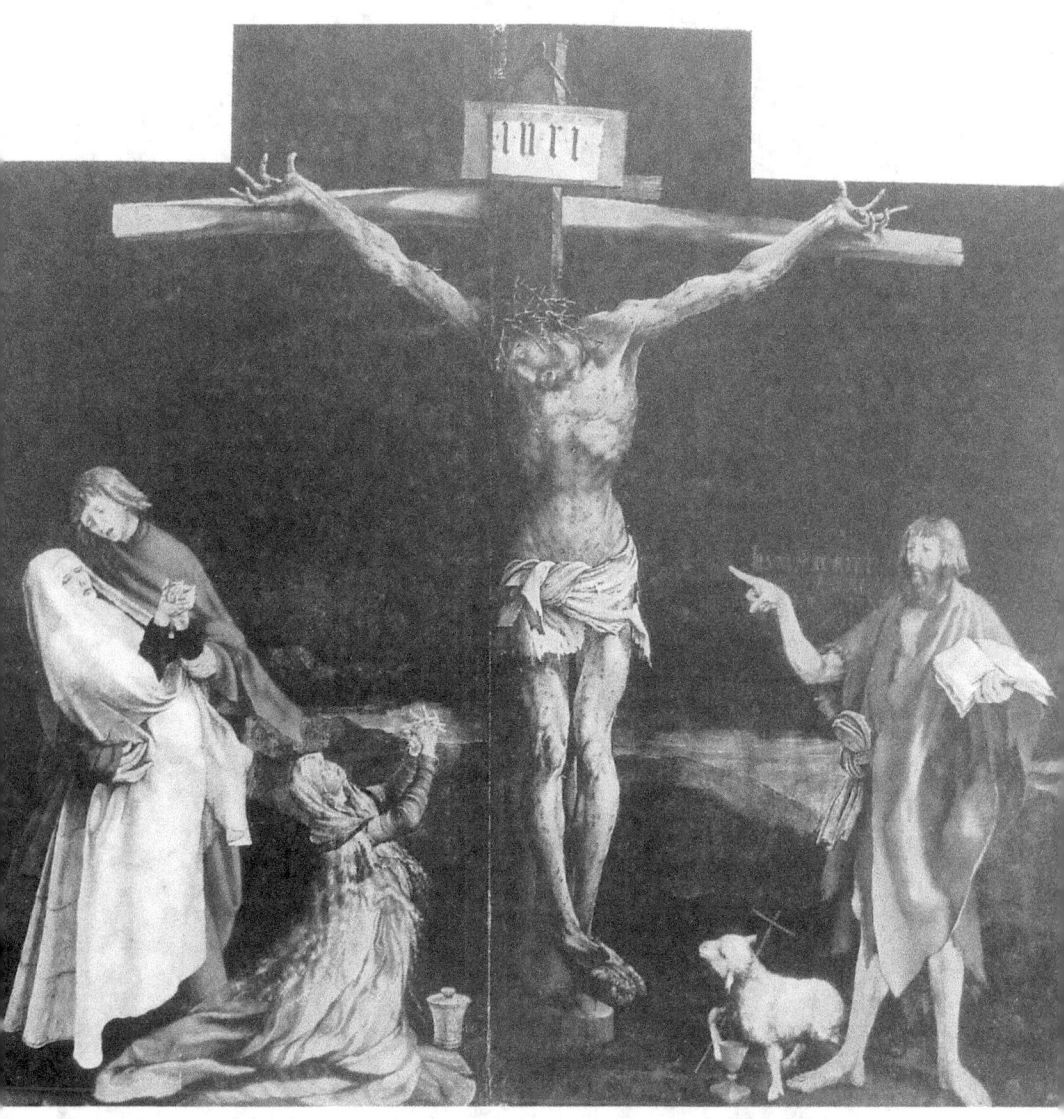

Matthias Grünewald, Crucifixion, Isenheim Altarpiece

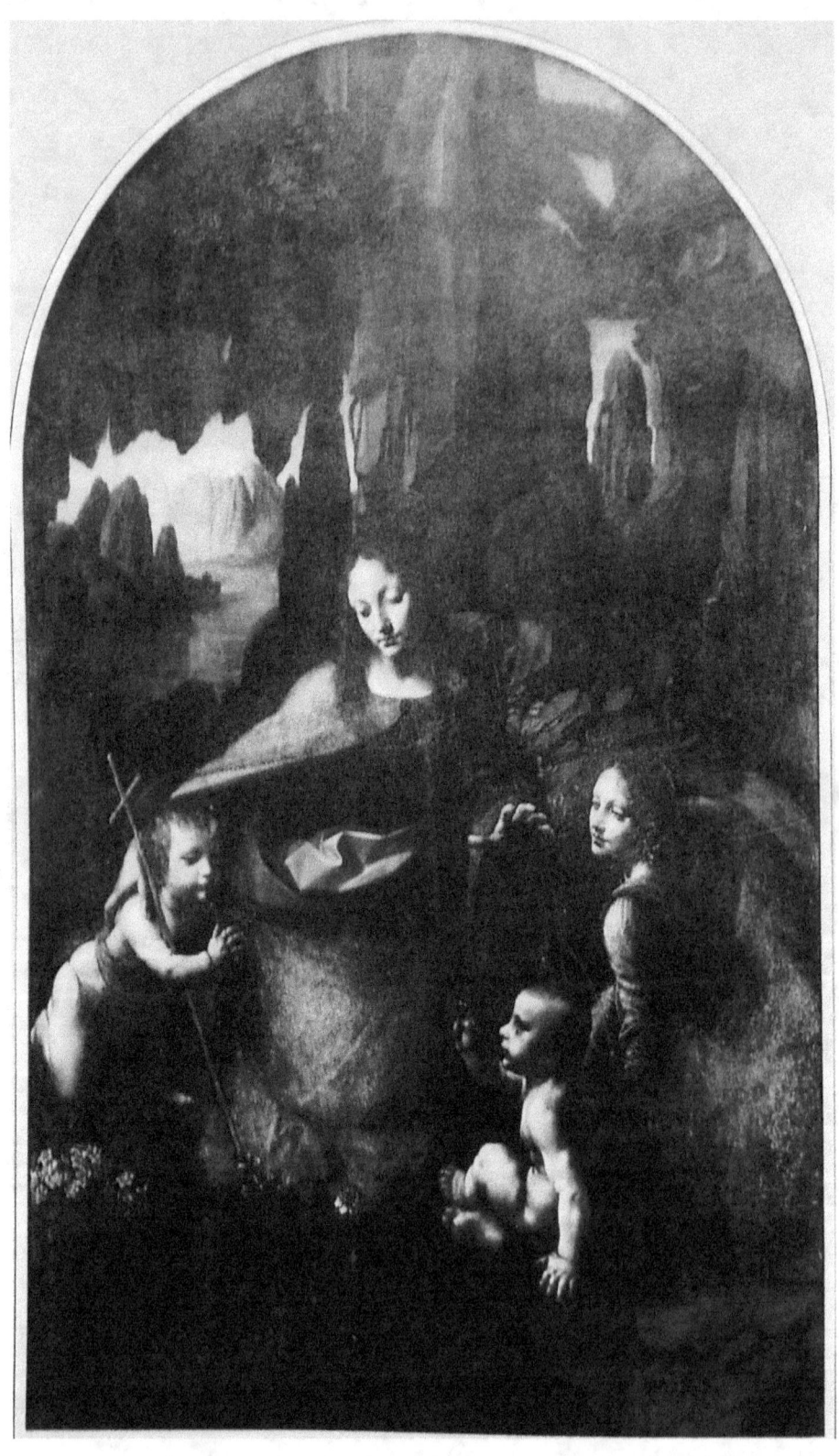

Leonardo da Vinci, The Madonna of the Rocks, London

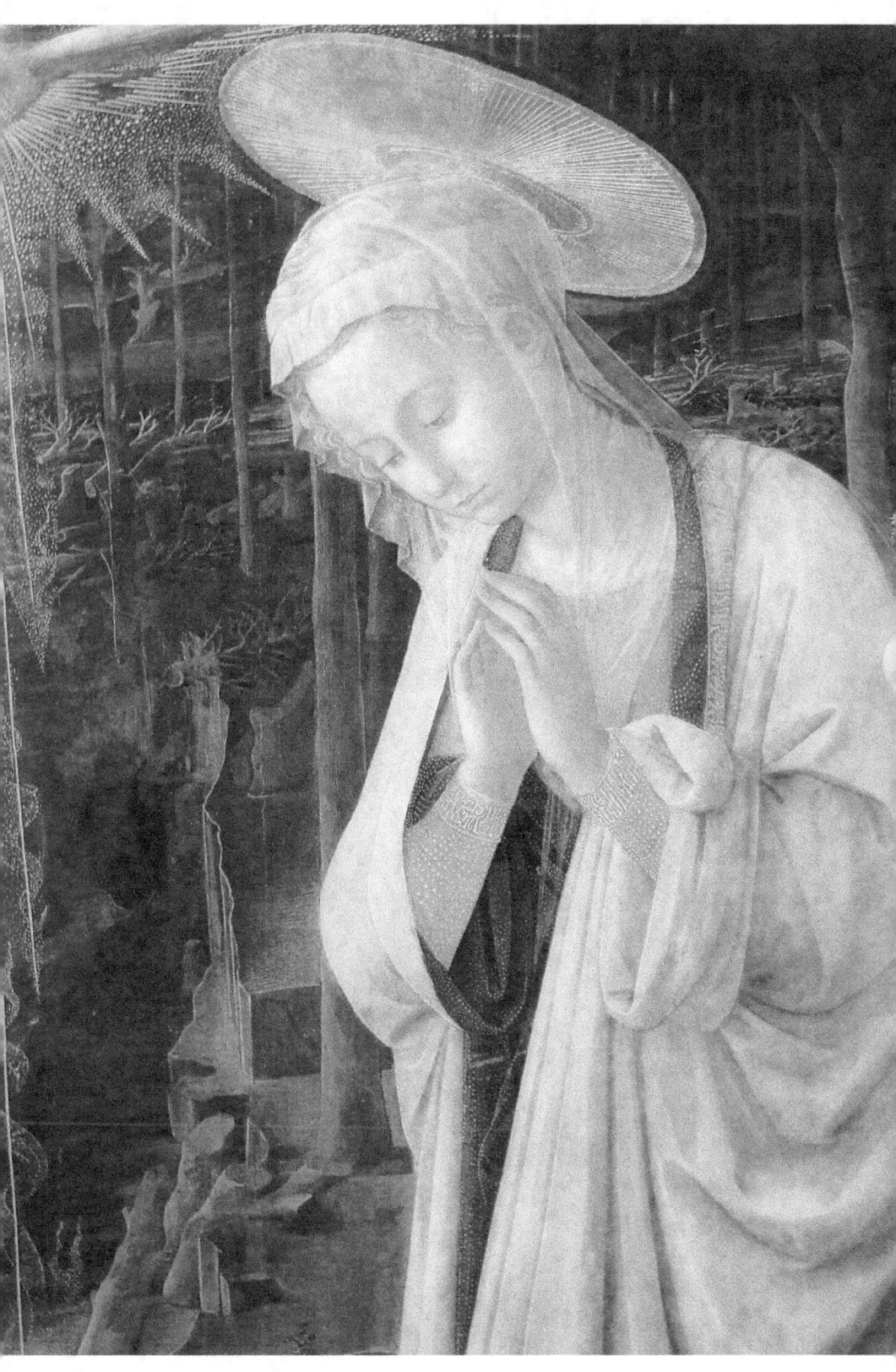

Fra Filippo Lippi, The Adoration of the Virgin, Berlin, detail

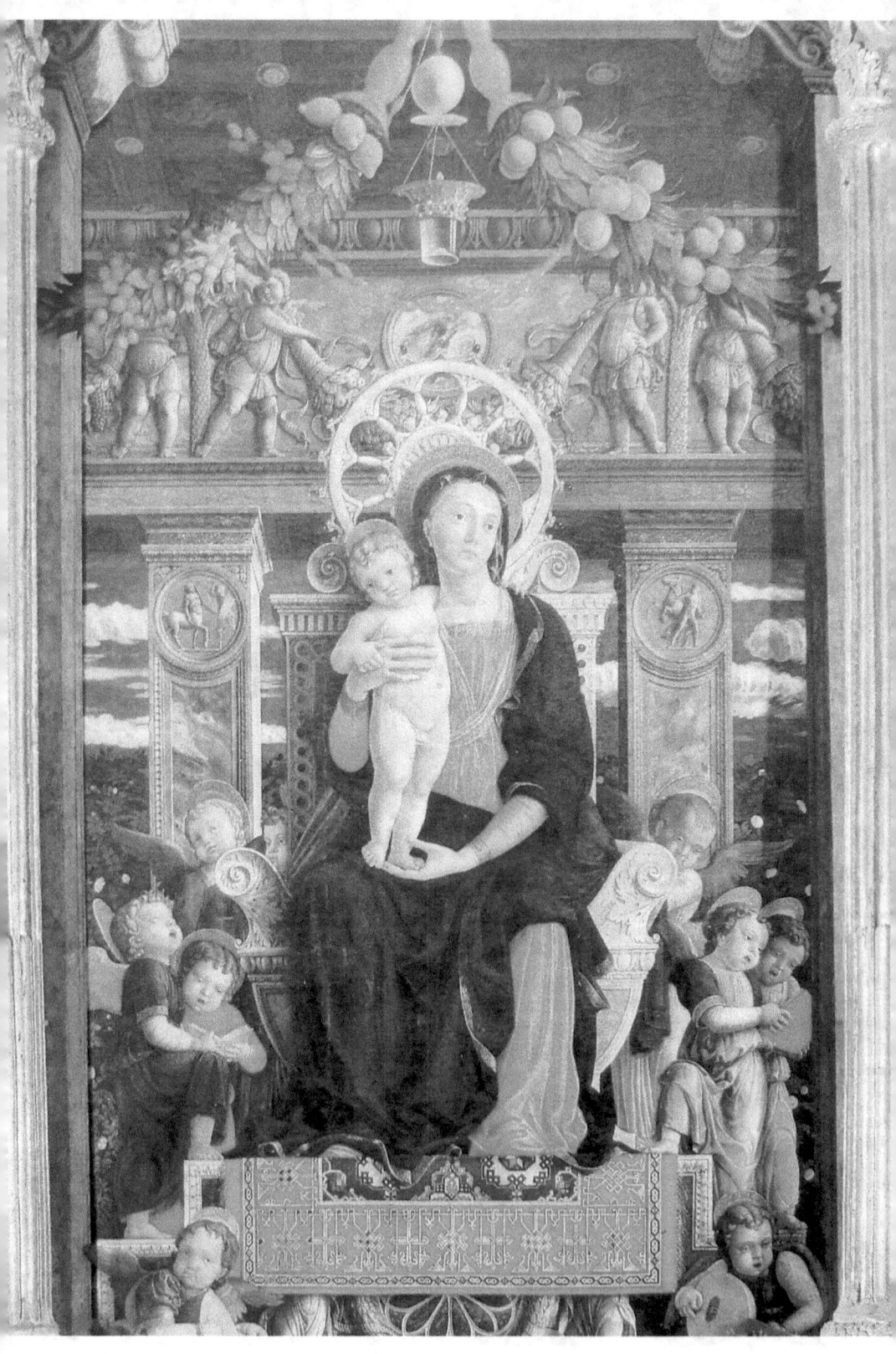

Andreas Mantegna, Madonna and Child Enthroned, 1457-60, Verona

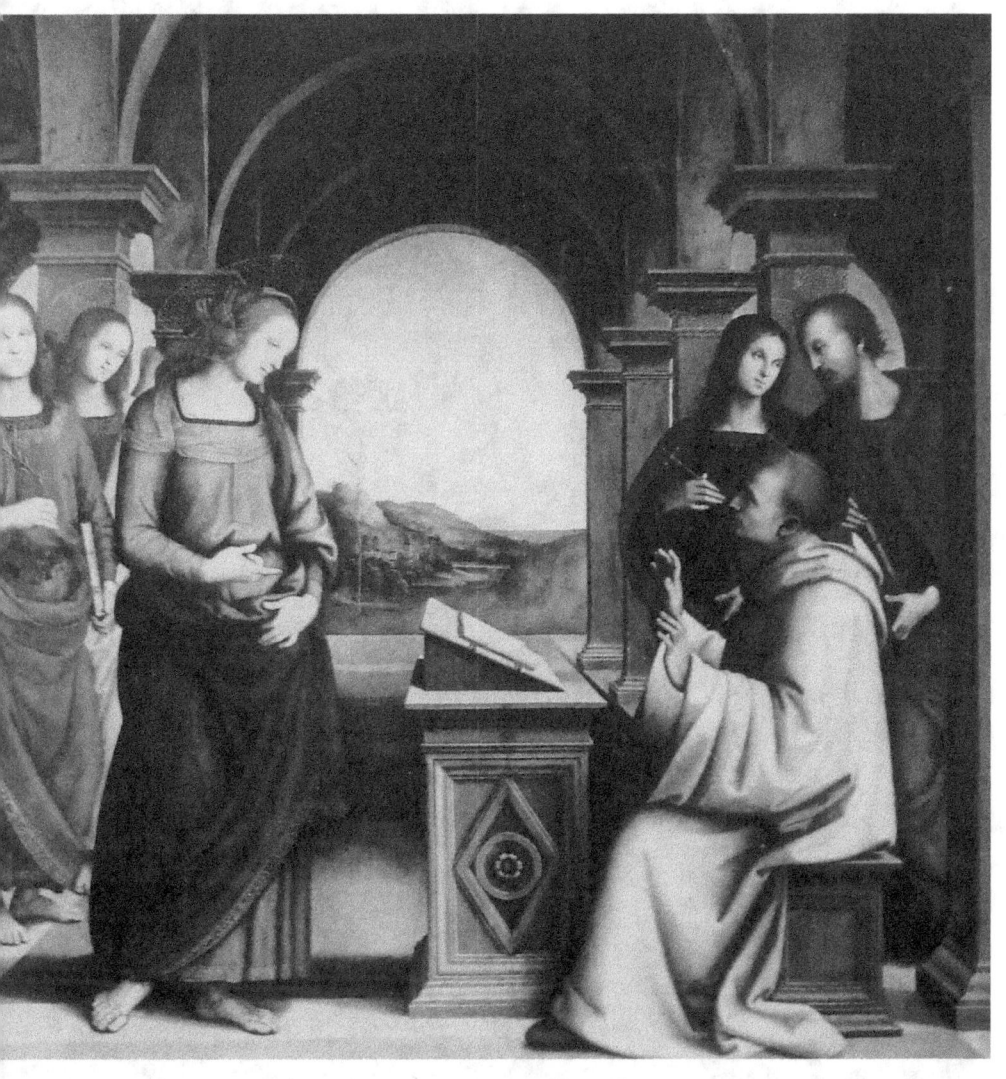

Perugino, Vision of St Bernard, 1488

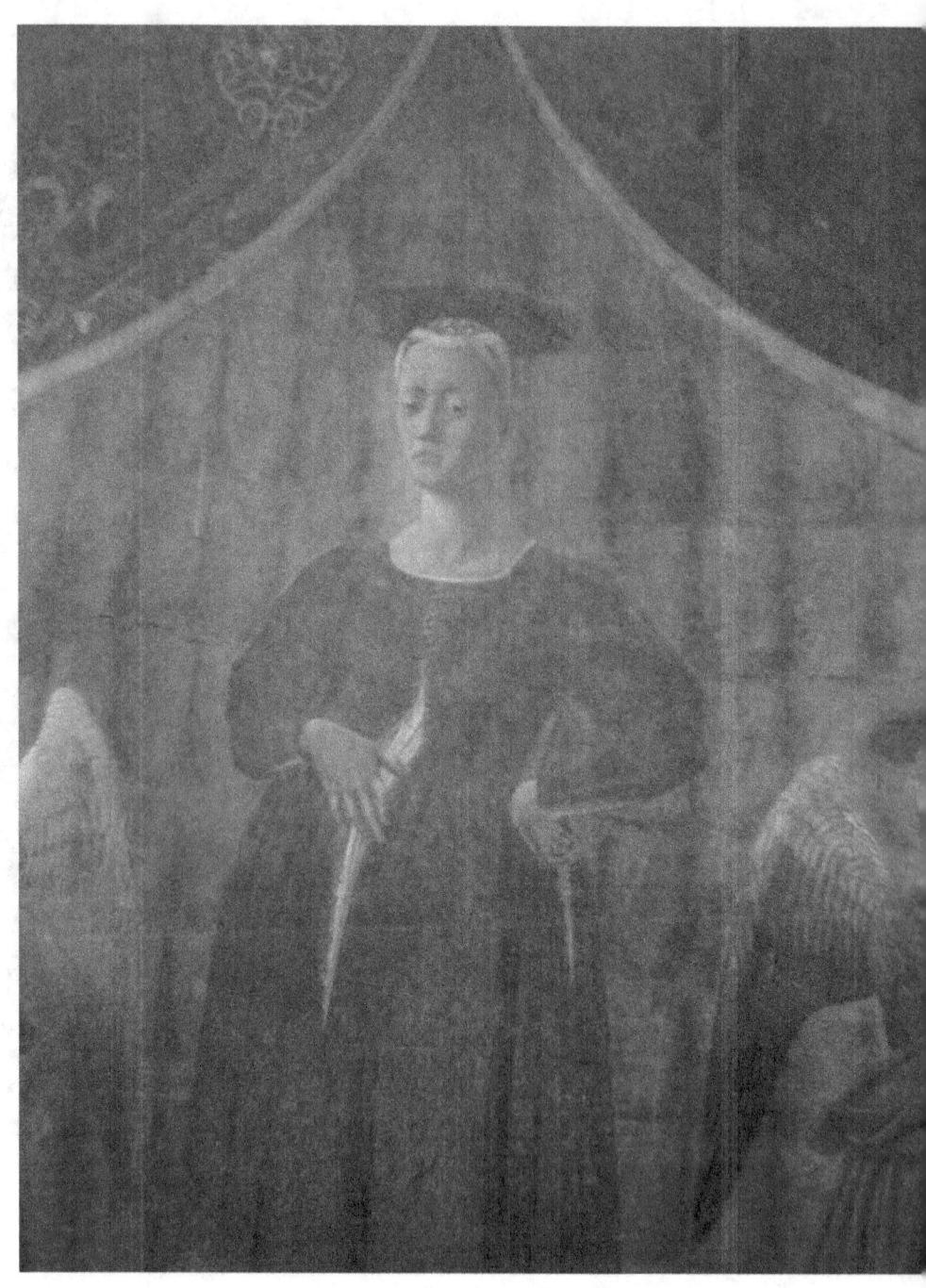

Piero della Francesca, Madonna del Parto

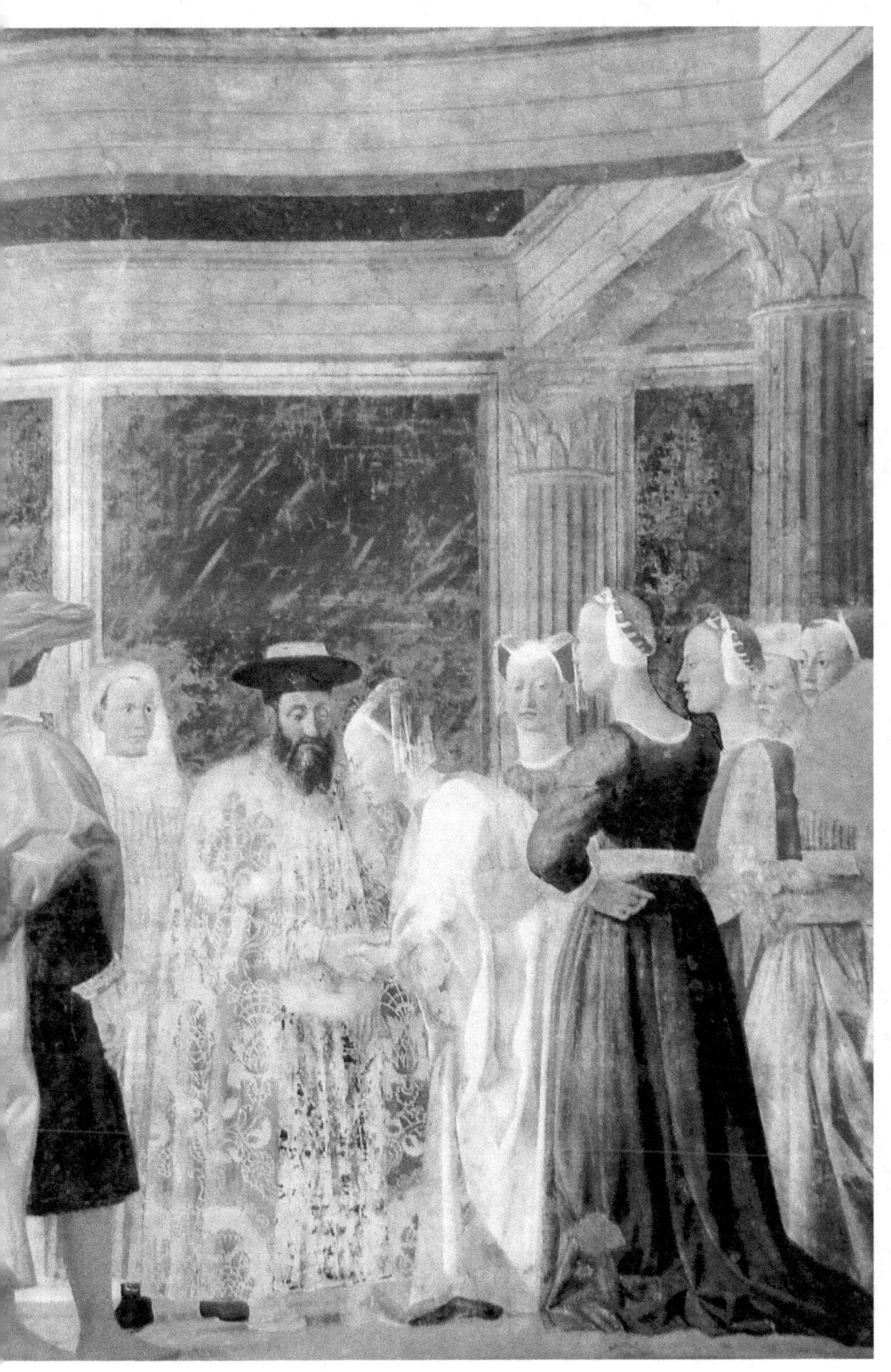

Piero della Francesca, frescoes, Arezzo

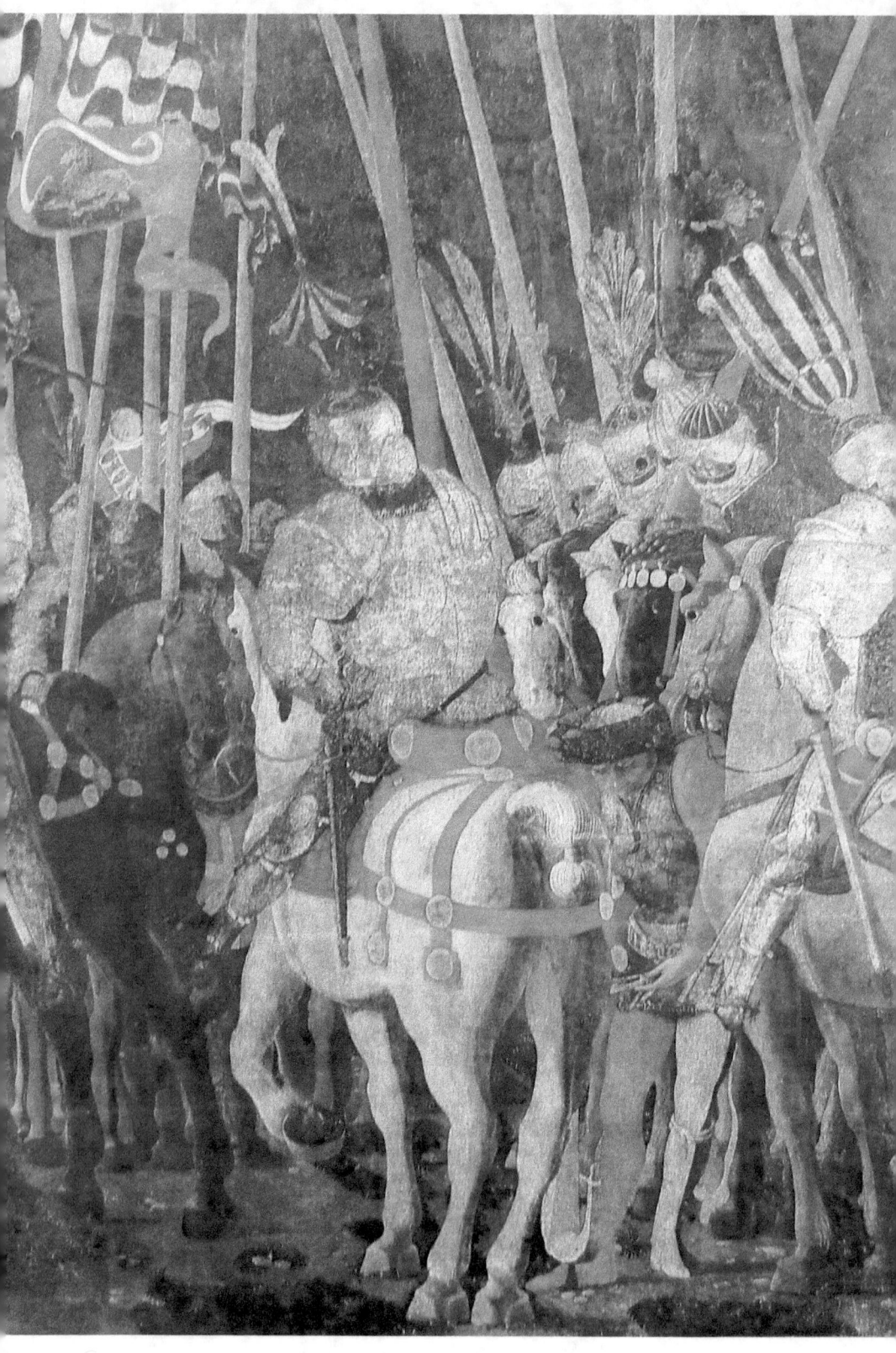

Paolo Uccello, The Battle of San Romano, Paris

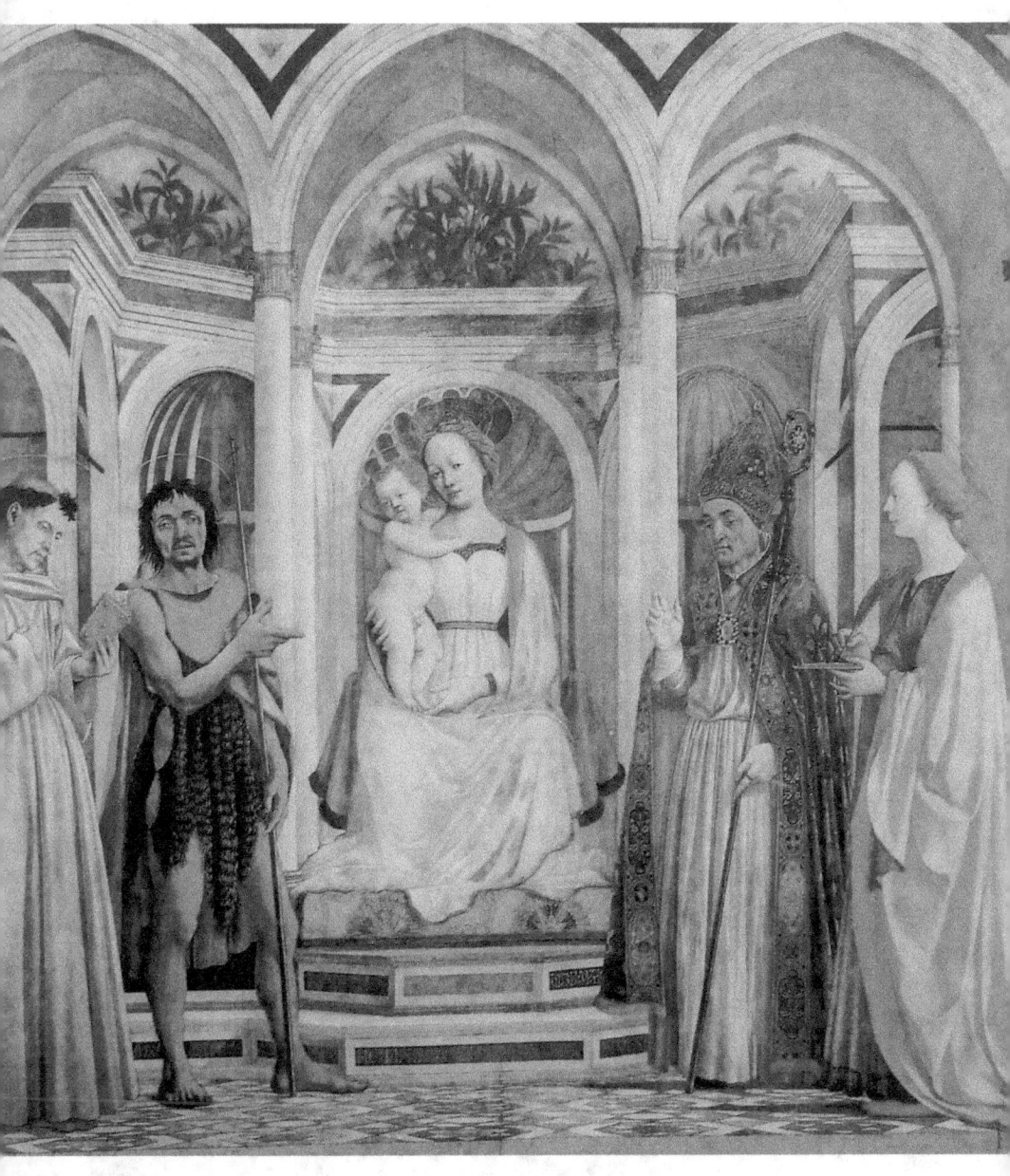

Domenico Veneziano, Madonna and Child With Saints, 1445, Uffizi Gallery

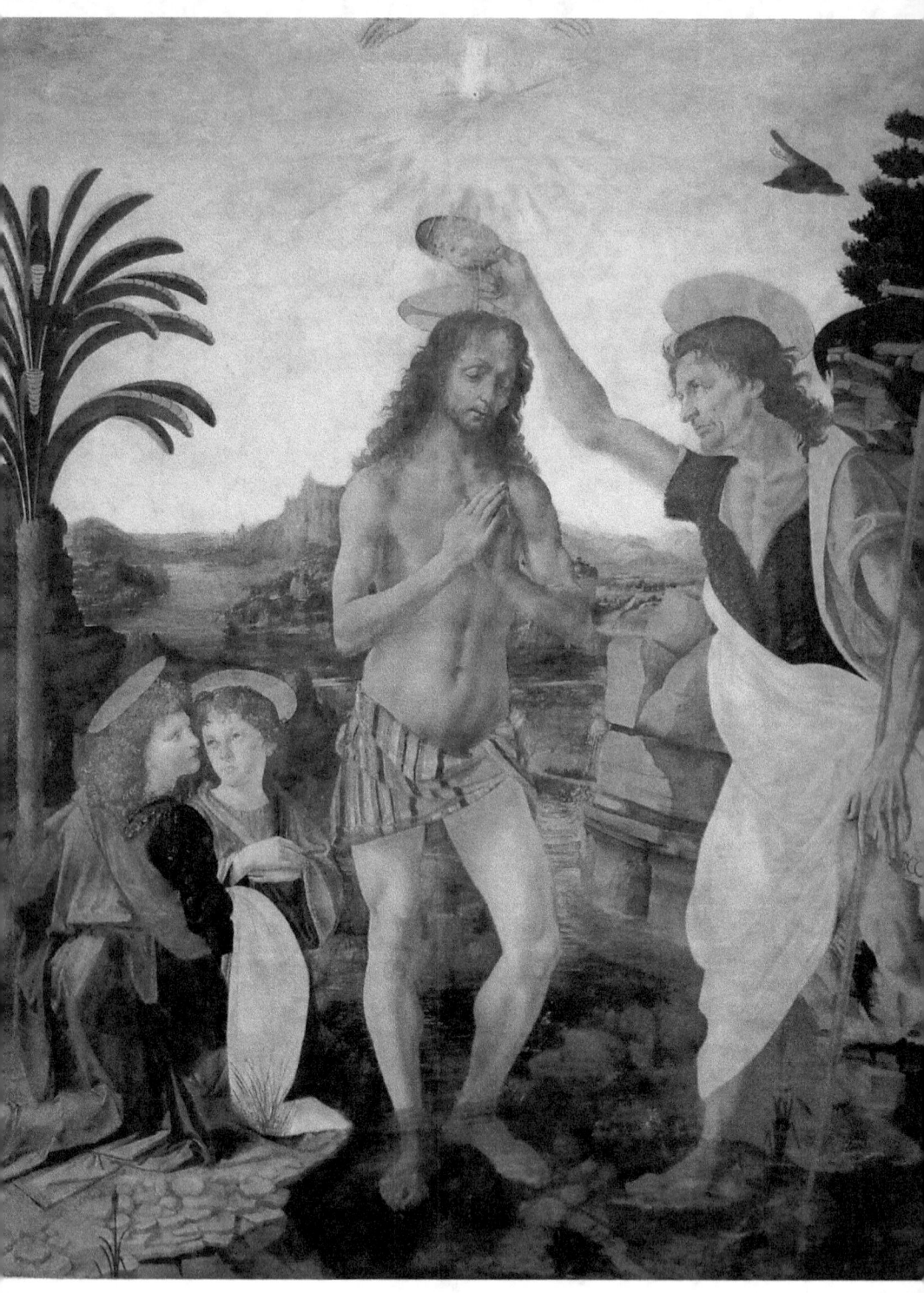

Andrea del Verrocchio, The Baptism of Christ

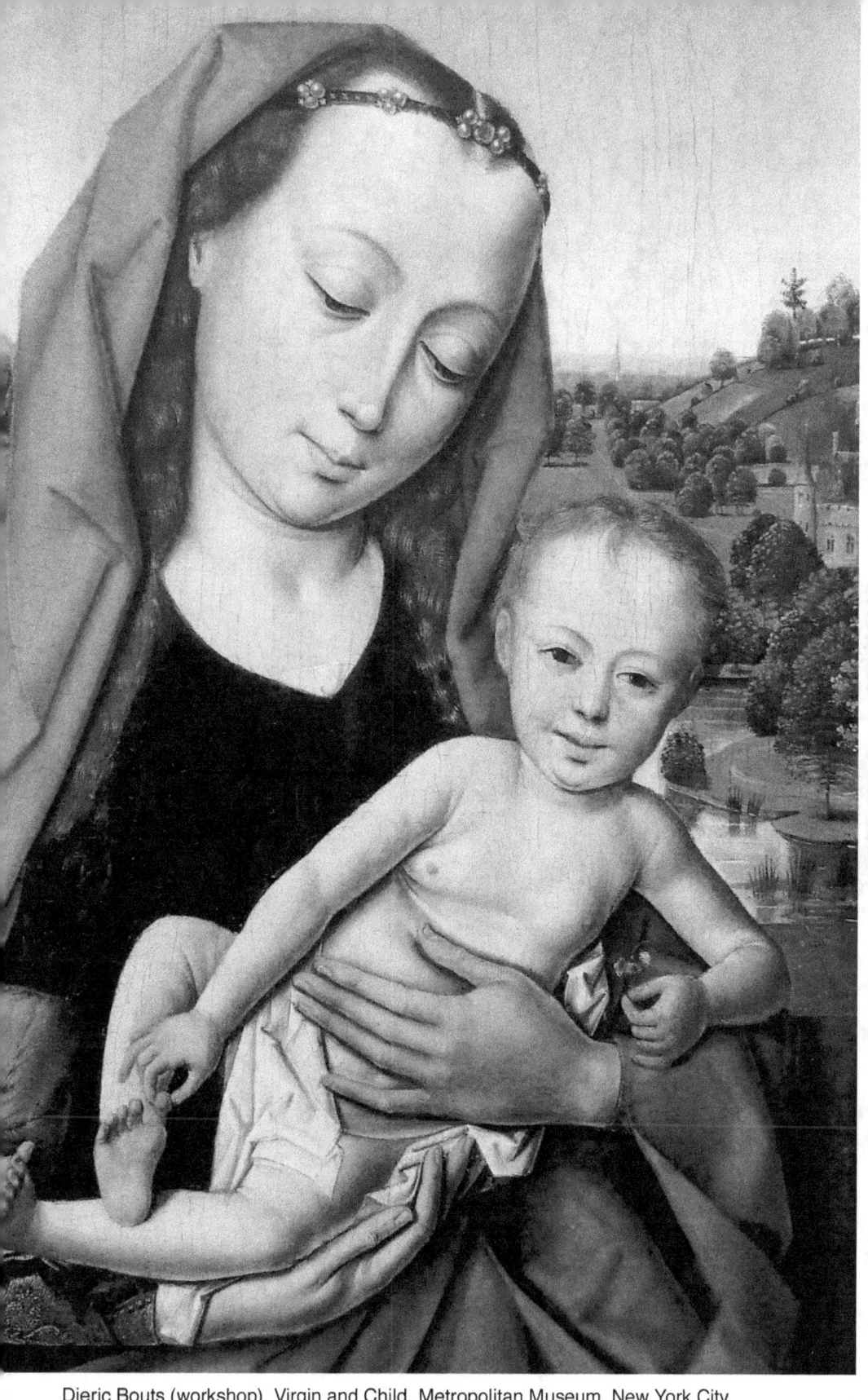

Dieric Bouts (workshop), Virgin and Child, Metropolitan Museum, New York City

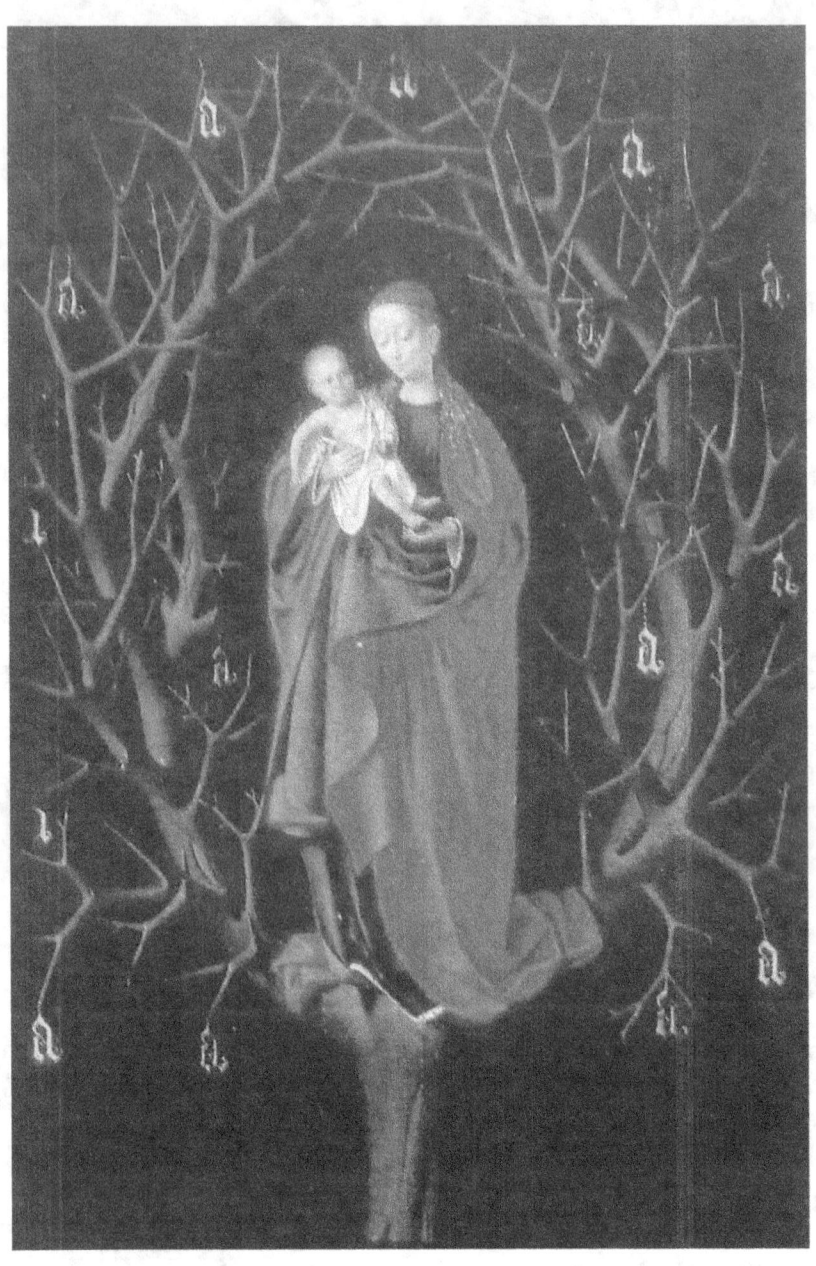

Petrus Christus, Madonna In a Barren Tree, 1450,
Prado, Madrid

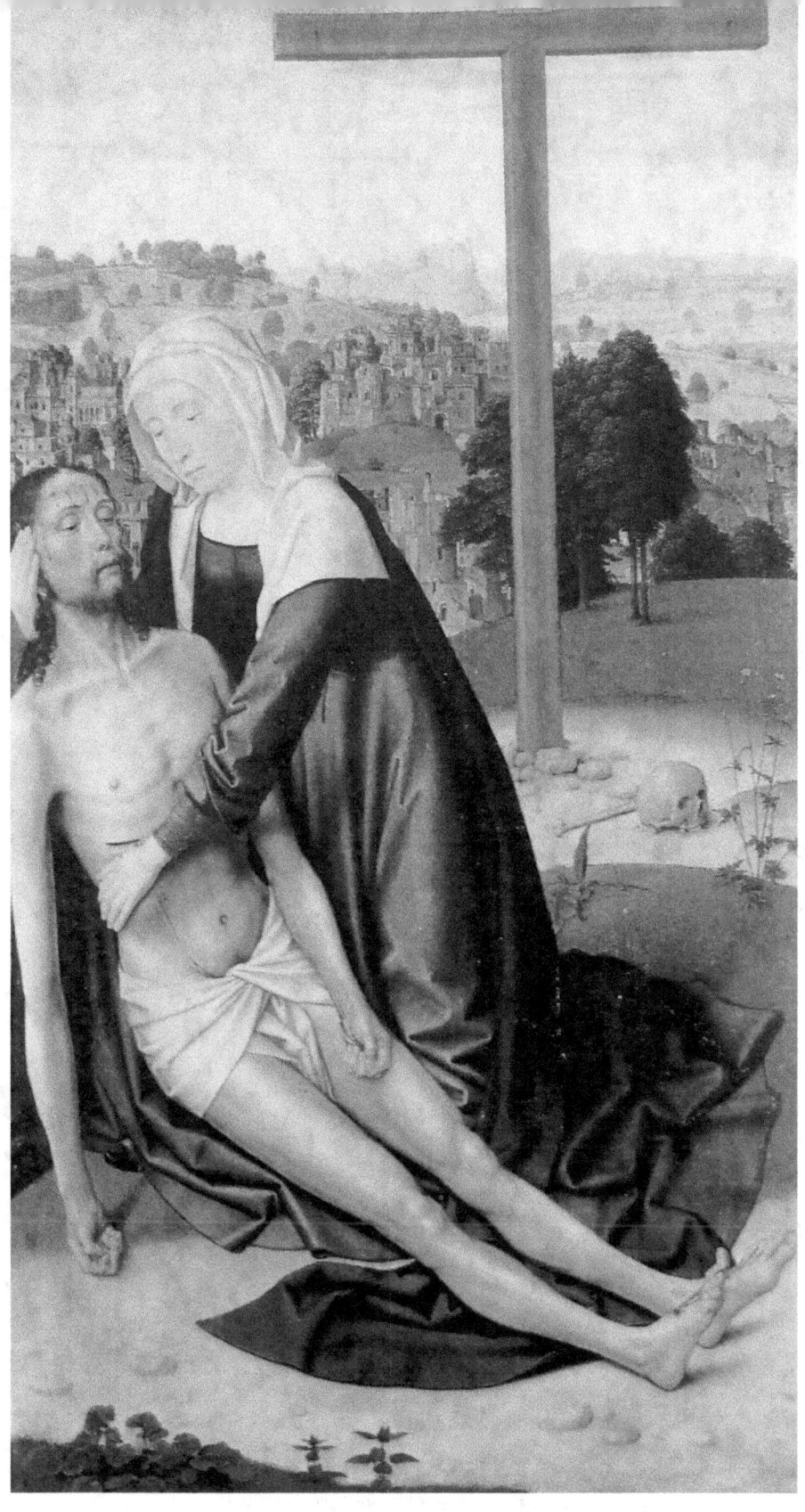

Gerard David, Pietà, Winterhur

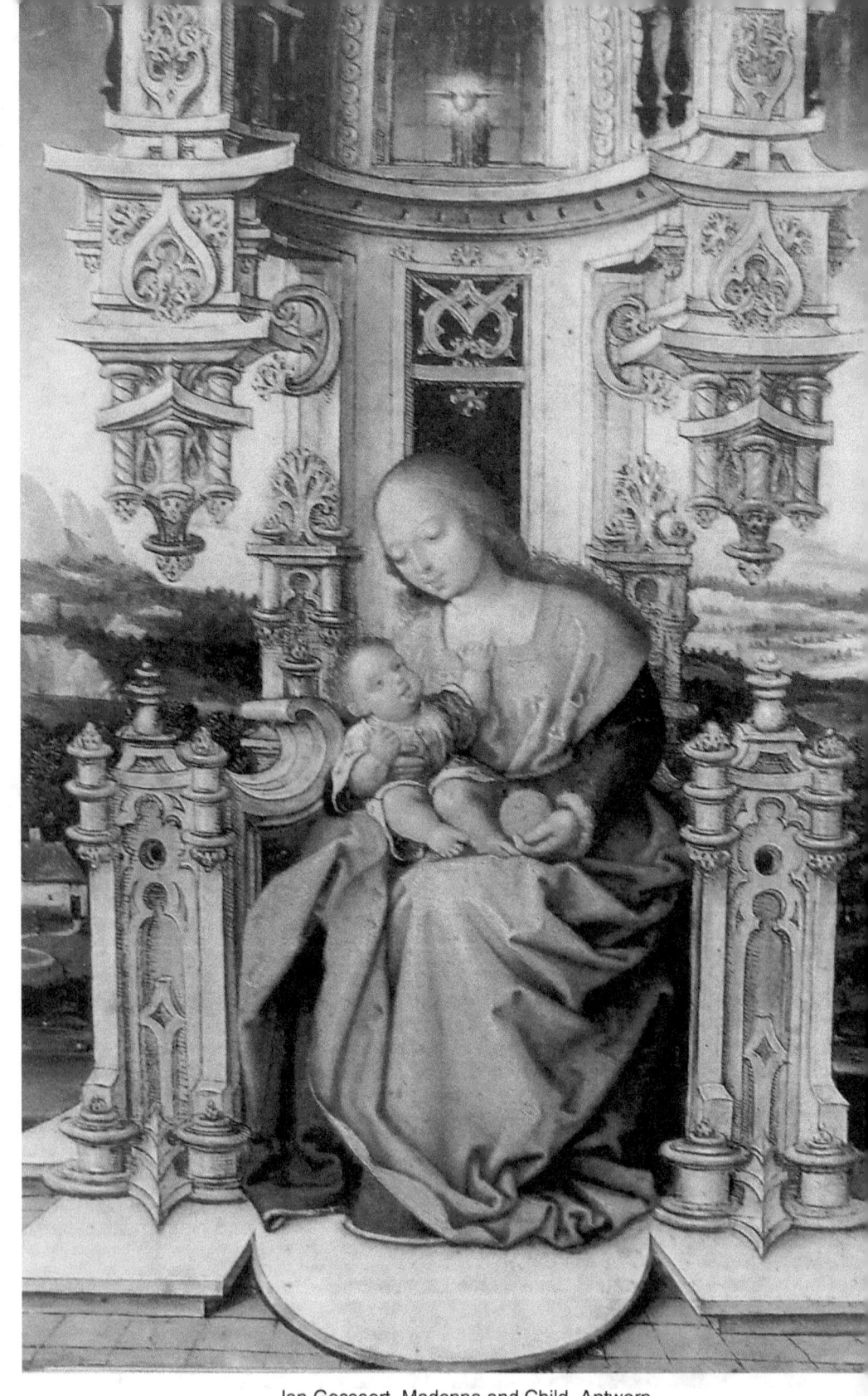

Jan Gossaert, Madonna and Child, Antwerp

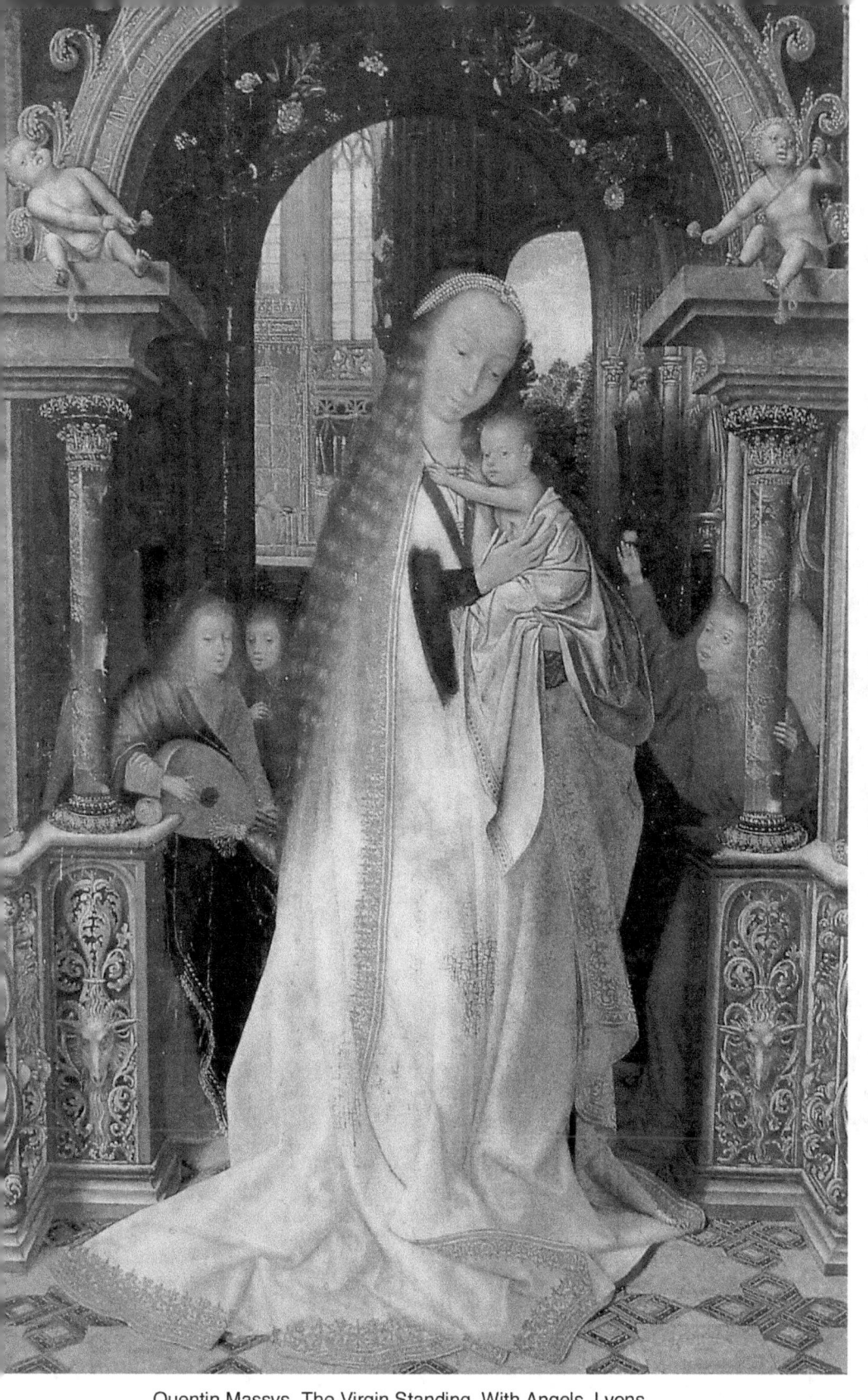

Quentin Massys, The Virgin Standing, With Angels, Lyons

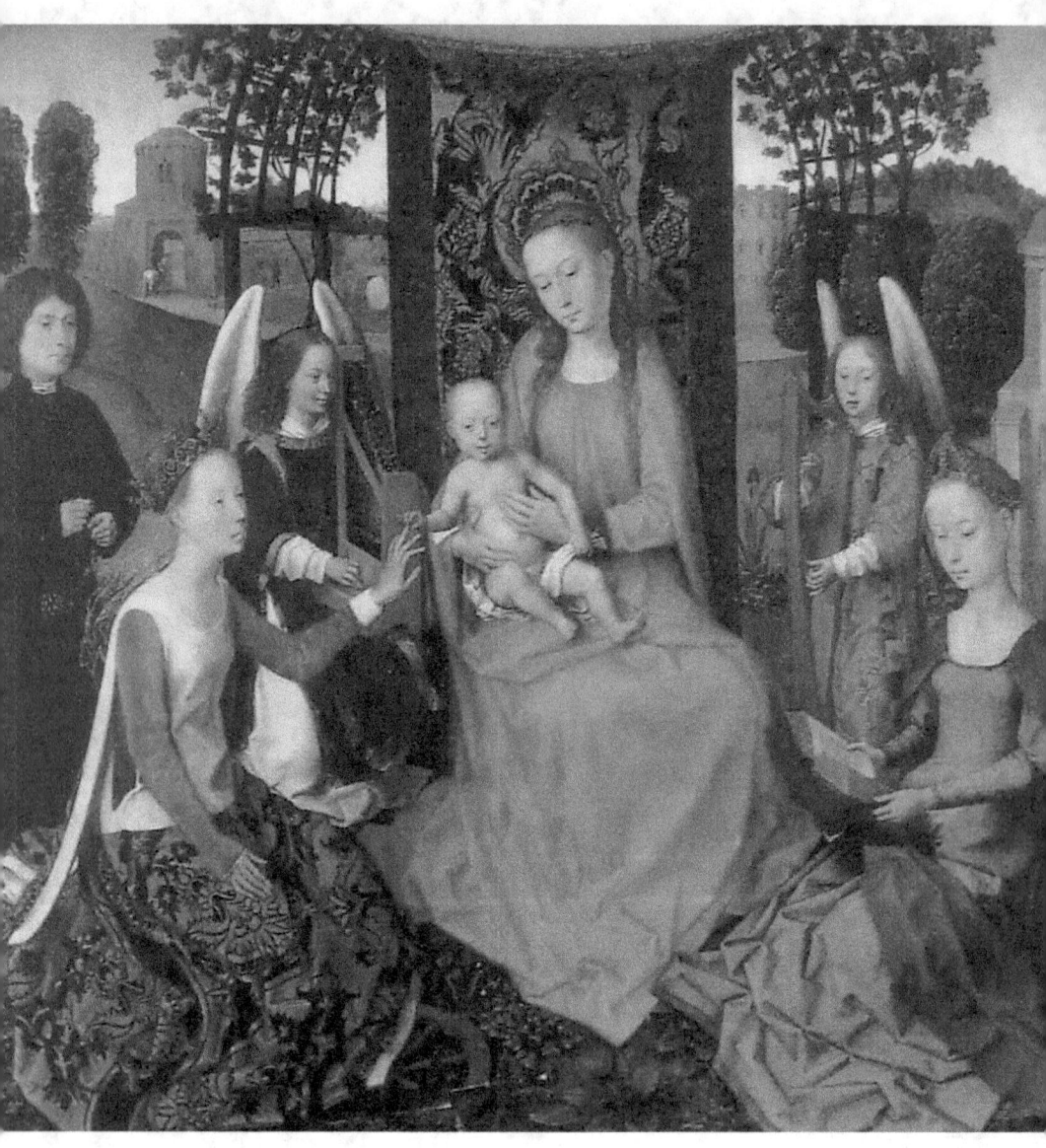

Hans Memling, The Mystic Marriage of St Catherine, Metropolitan
Museum, New York City

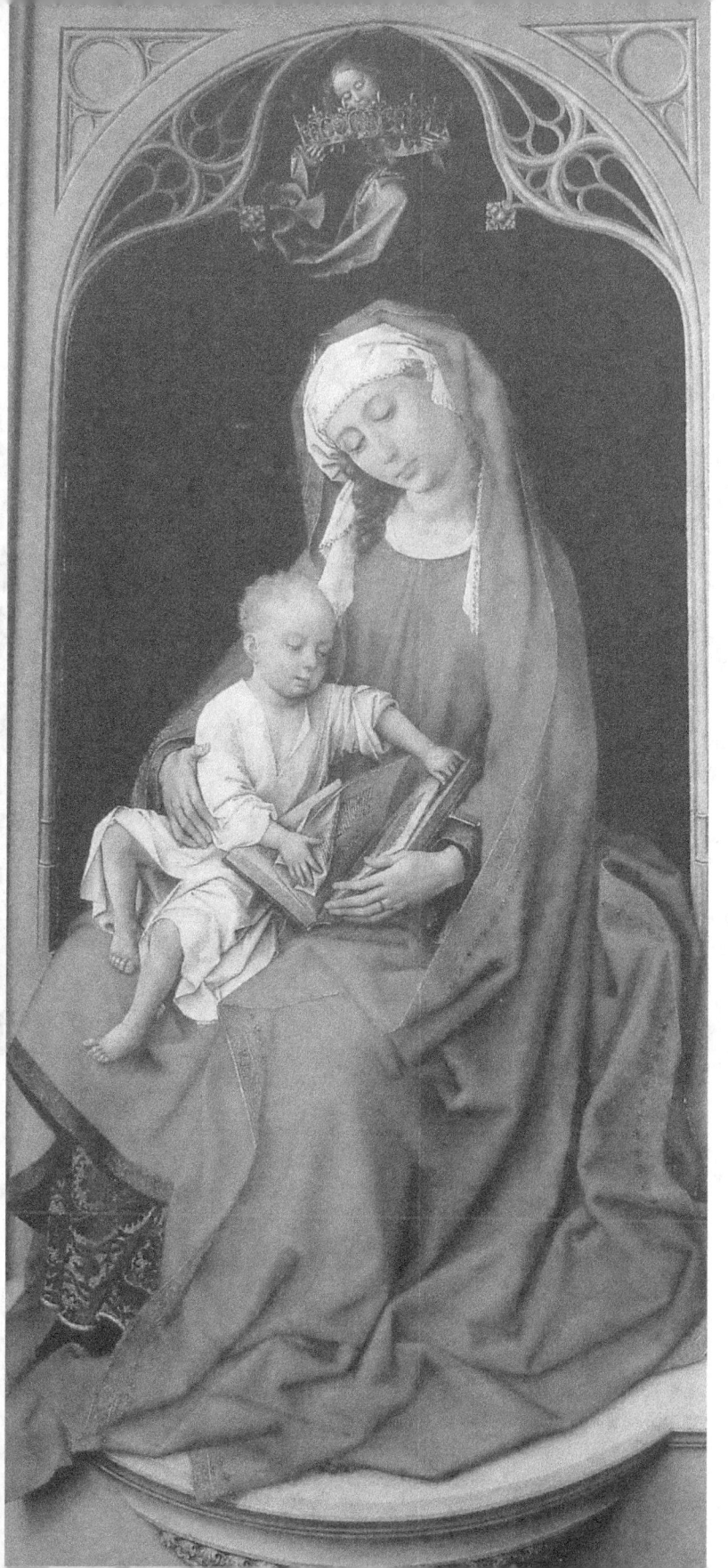

Rogier van der
Weyden,
Madonna and
Child, Prado,
Madrid

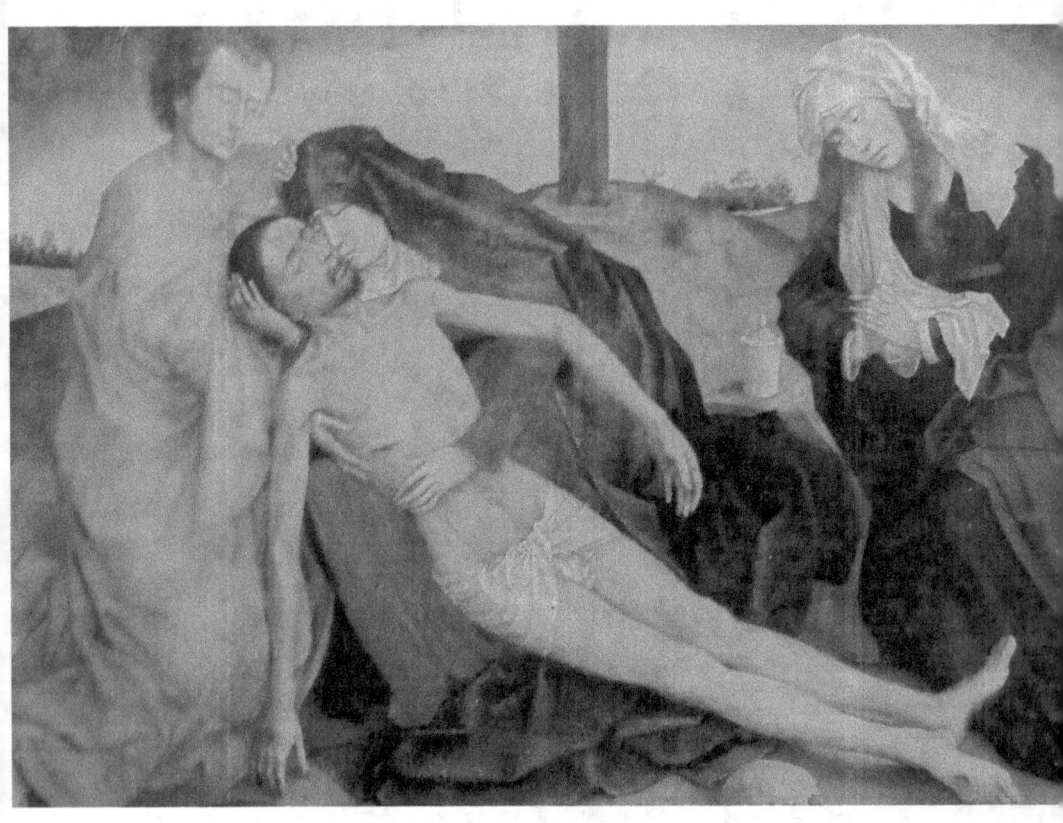

Rogier van der Weyden, Pietà, Brussels

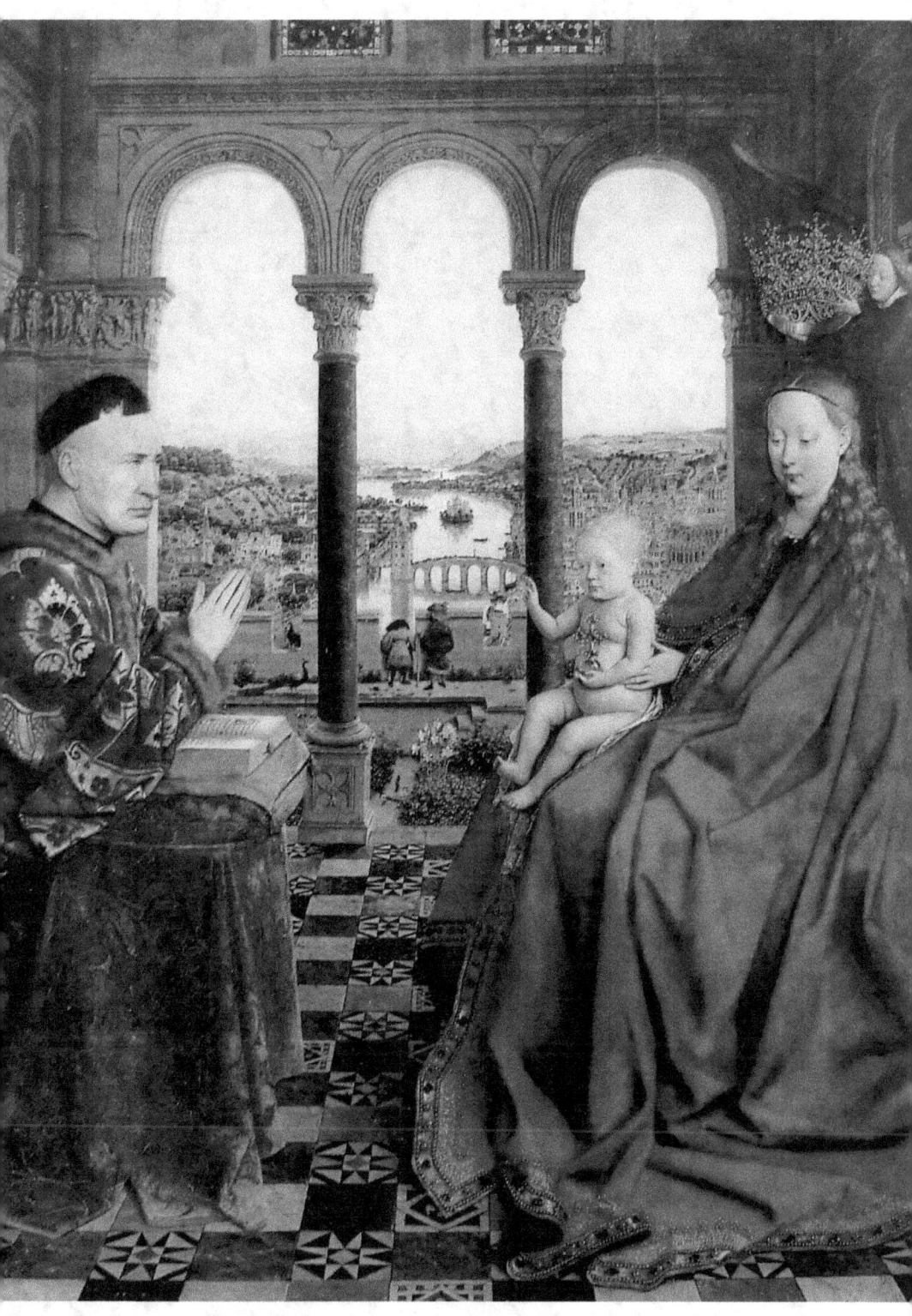

Jan van Eyck, The Rolin Madonna, Louvre, Paris

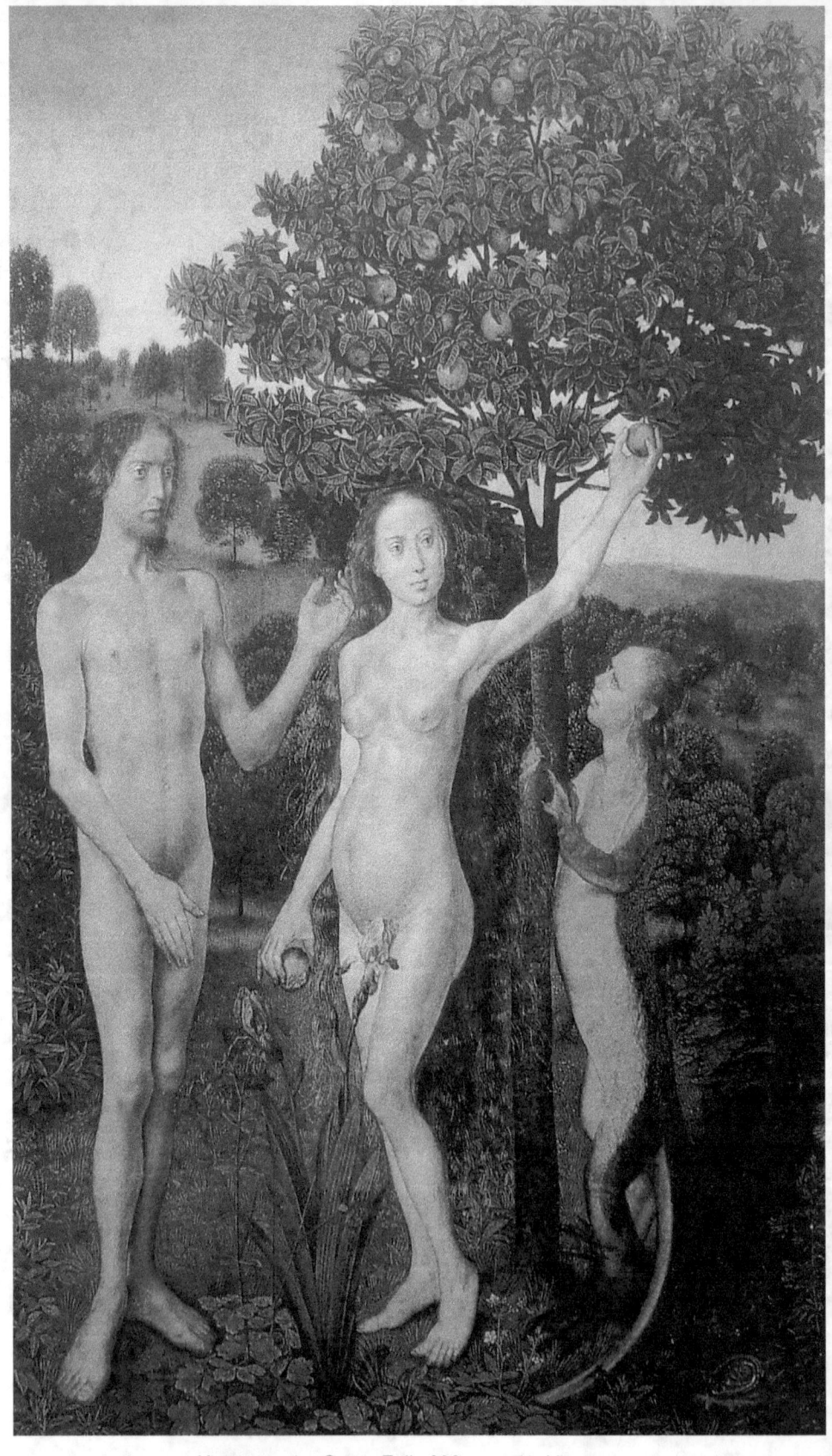

Hugo van der Goes, Fall of Man, 1470, Vienna

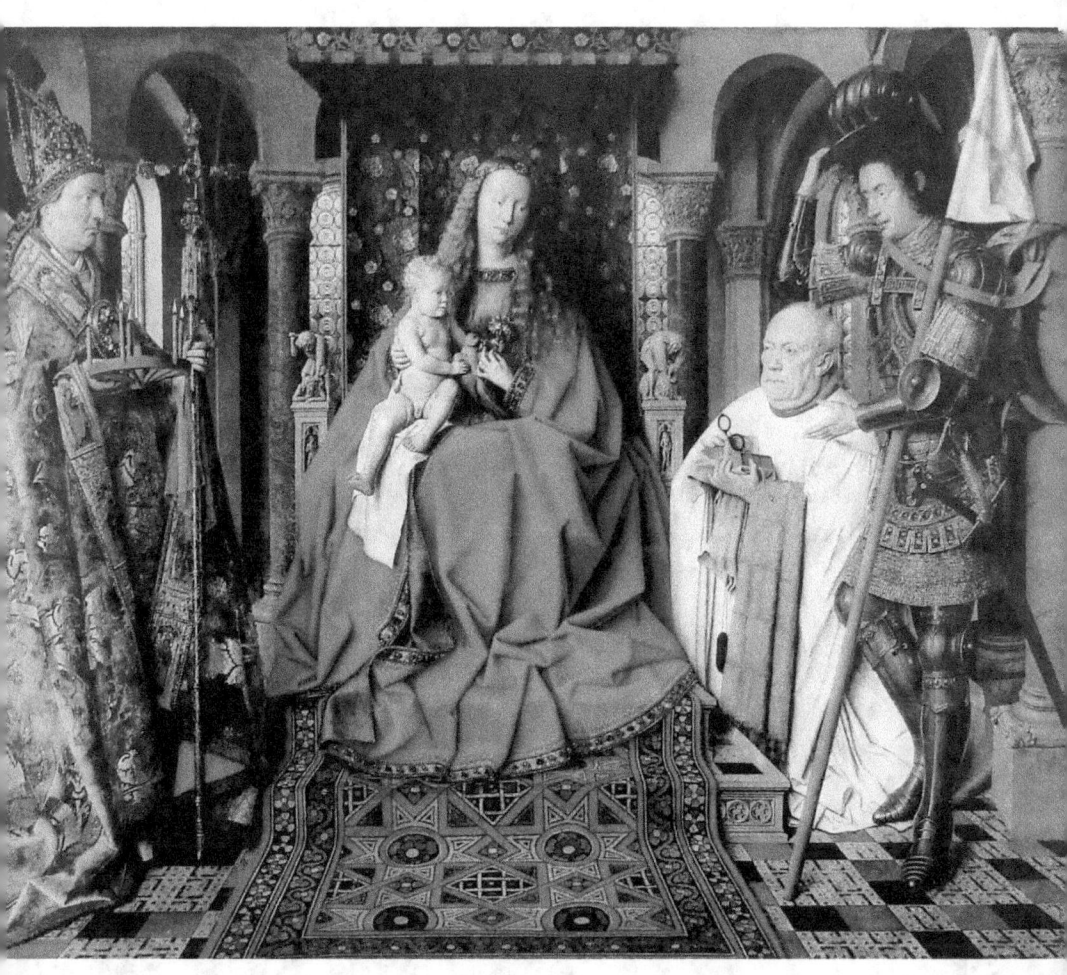

Jan van Eyck, The Paele Madonna, 1436, Bruges

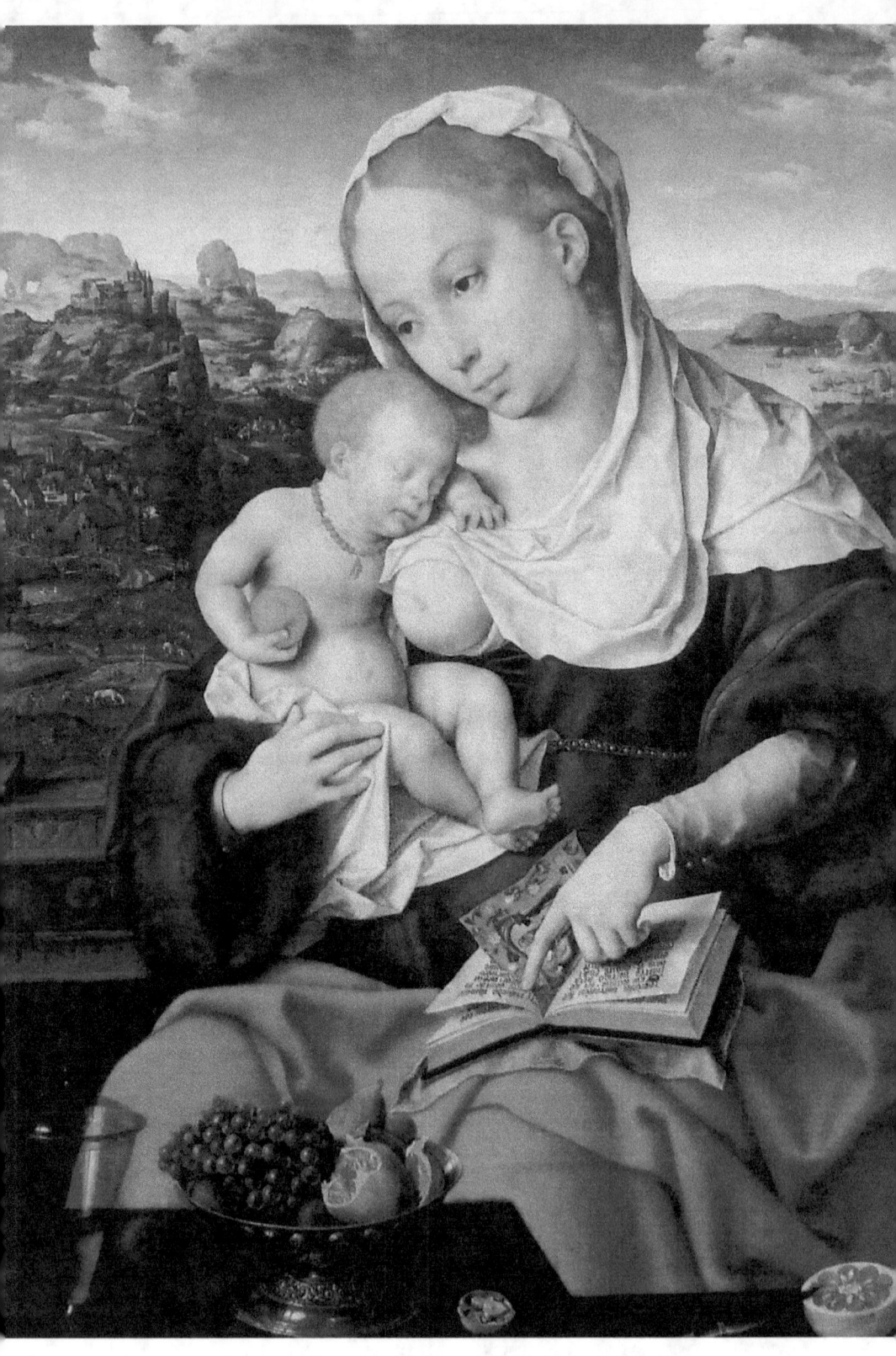

Joos van Cleve, Madonna and Child, Metropolitan Museum,
New York City

THE ART OF
ANDY GOLDSWORTHY

COMPLETE WORKS: SPECIAL EDITION
(PAPERBACK and HARDBACK)

by William Malpas

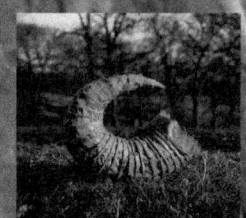

A new, special edition of the study of the contemporary British sculptor,
Andy Goldsworthy, including a new introduction, new bibliography and many
new illustrations.

This is the most comprehensive, up-to-date, well-researched and in-depth
account of Goldsworthy's art available anywhere.

Andy Goldsworthy makes land art. His sculpture is a sensitive, intuitive
response to nature, light, time, growth, the seasons and the earth. Goldsworthy's environmental art is becoming ever more popular: 1993's art book
Stone was a bestseller; the press raved about Goldsworthy taking over a
number of London West End art galleries in 1994; during 1995 Goldsworthy
designed a set of Royal Mail stamps and had a show at the British Museum.
Malpas surveys all of Goldsworthy's art, and analyzes his relation with other
land artists such as Robert Smithson, Walter de Maria, Richard Long and
David Nash, and his place in the contemporary British art scene.

The Art of Andy Goldsworthy discusses all of Goldsworthy's important and
recent exhibitions and books, including the *Sheepfolds* project; the TV docu-
mentaries; *Wood* (1996); the New York Holocaust memorial (2003); and
Goldsworthy's collaboration on a dance performance.

Illustrations: 70 b/w, 1 colour. 330 pages. New, special, 2nd edition.
Publisher: Crescent Moon Publishing. Distributor: Gardners Books.

ISBN 1-86171-059-3 (9781861710598) (Paperback) £25.00 / $44.00

ISBN 1-86171-080-1 (9781861710802) (Hardback) £60.00 / $105.00

ANDY GOLDSWORTHY
IN CLOSE-UP

SPECIAL EDITION (HARDBACK and PAPERBACK)

by William Malpas

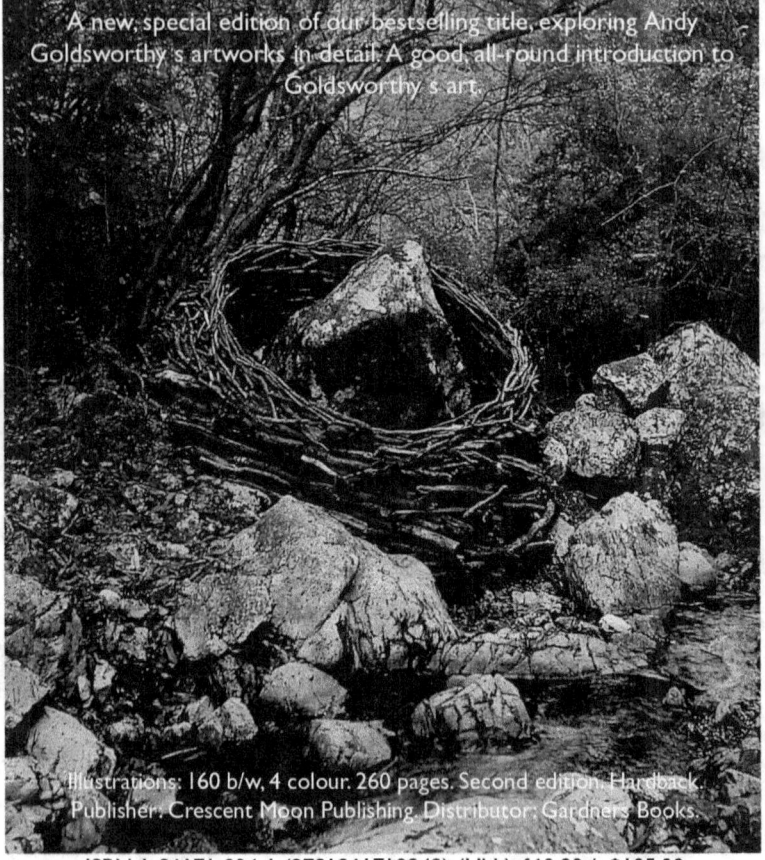

A new, special edition of our bestselling title, exploring Andy Goldsworthy's artworks in detail. A good, all-round introduction to Goldsworthy's art.

Illustrations: 160 b/w, 4 colour. 260 pages. Second edition. Hardback. Publisher: Crescent Moon Publishing. Distributor: Gardners Books.

ISBN 1-86171-094-1 (9781861710949) (Hbk) £60.00 / $105.00

ISBN 1-86171-091-7 (9781861710919) (Pbk) £25.00 / $44.00

Available from bookstores. amazon.com, play.com, tesco.com, and other web-sites.
In the United States from Baker & Taylor, (800) 7753760 or (800) 7751100 or (908) 5417062. electser@btol.com or btinfo@btol.com.

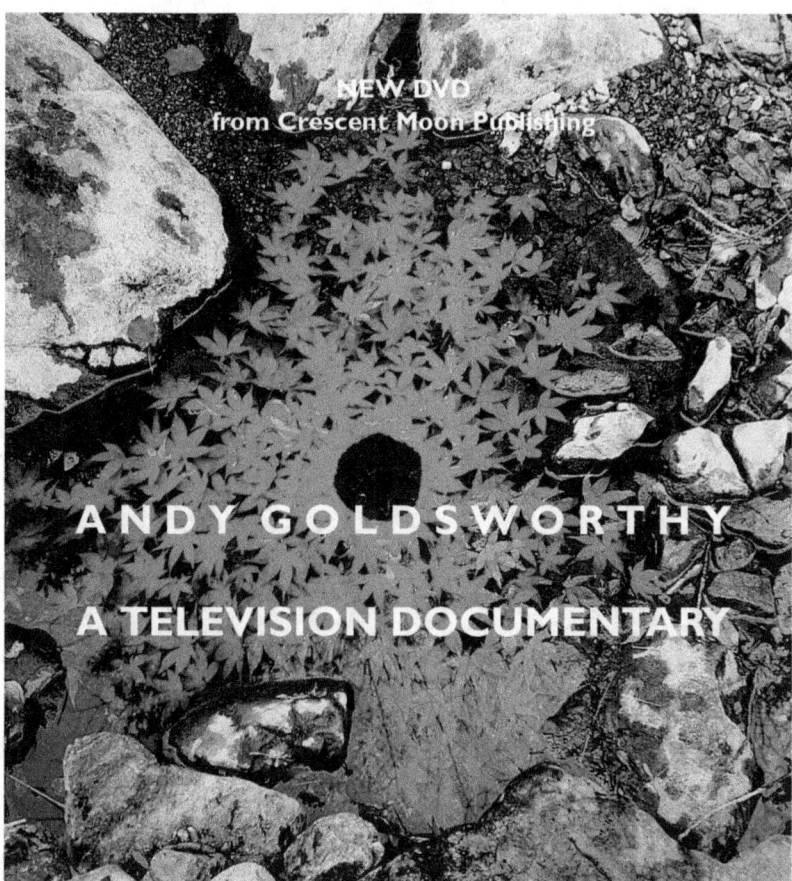

ANDY GOLDSWORTHY

A TELEVISION DOCUMENTARY

Andy Goldsworthy makes land art. His sculpture is a sensitive, intuitive response to nature, light, time, growth, the seasons and the earth. Goldsworthy's environmental art is becoming ever more popular: his art books are bestsellers; he has exhibited around the world; important and recent exhibitions include the Sheepfolds project; the Washington installation (2005); Passage (2004); the New York Holocaust memorial (2003); and a collaboration on a dance performance.

This video documentary surveys every aspect of Andy Goldsworthy's art, and all of his major works. It also discusses his relation with other land artists such as Robert Smithson, Walter de Maria, Richard Long and David Nash, and his place in the contemporary art scene in the UK.

This is the only TV documentary of its kind available on DVD and video.

EXTRAS

Resources: further reading; complete bibliography of Andy Goldsworthy, and life and work (on DVD-ROM); and weblinks.
Photo library of land artworks.
Extra footage.

55 minutes. PAL and NTSC. Colour. DVD. Multi-region. VHS video.
Stereo. E (Exempt from classification)

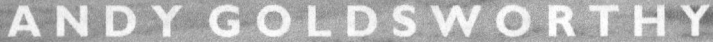

ANDY GOLDSWORTHY

TOUCHING NATURE:
SPECIAL EDITION

(PAPERBACK and HARDBACK)

by William Malpas

A new, special and updated edition of our bestselling title, providing
an excellent general introduction to the art of Andy Goldsworthy.

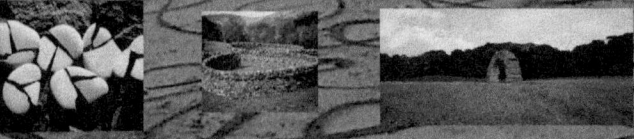

Illustrations: 75 b/w, 2 colour. 354 pages. Third edition. Paperback.

Publisher: Crescent Moon Publishing. Distributor: Gardners Books.

ISBN 1-86171-056-9 (9781861717) (Paperback) £25.00 / $44.00

ISBN 1-86171-087-9 (9781861710871) (Hardback) £60.00 / $105.00

LAND ART

A COMPLETE GUIDE TO LANDSCAPE, ENVIRONMENTAL, EARTHWORKS, NATURE, SCULPTURE AND INSTALLATION ART

by William Malpas

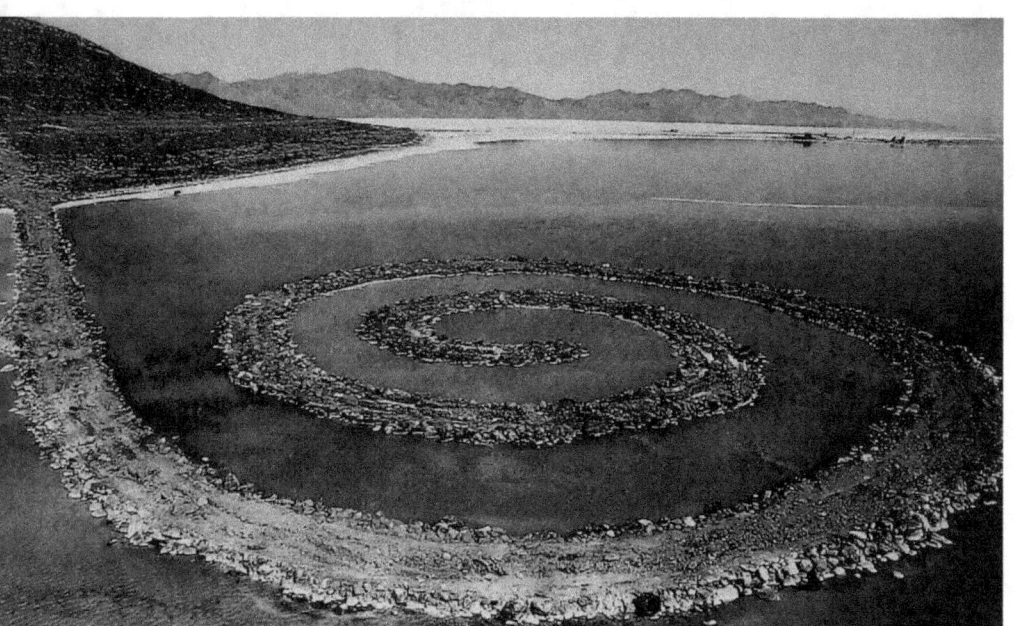

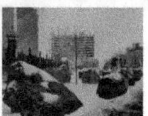 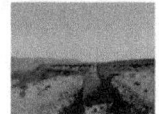 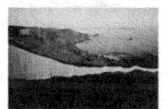 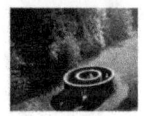 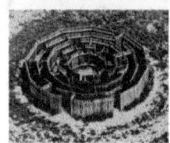

A new, special edition of our popular book on land art.
Chapters on land artists such as Robert Smithson, Walter de Maria, Christo,
Michael Heizer, Richard Long and Andy Goldsworthy.

Illustrations: 35 b/w, 2 colour. 314 pages. First edition. Paperback.

Publisher: Crescent Moon Publishing. Distributor: Gardners Books.

ISBN 1-86171-062-3 (9781861710628) £25.00 / $44.00

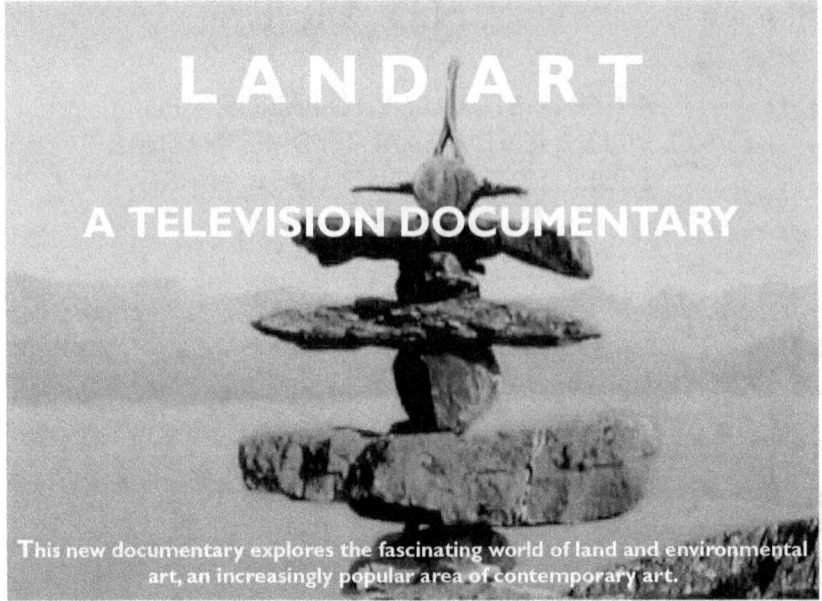

LAND ART IN CLOSE-UP

SPECIAL EDITION (PAPERBACK)

by William Malpas

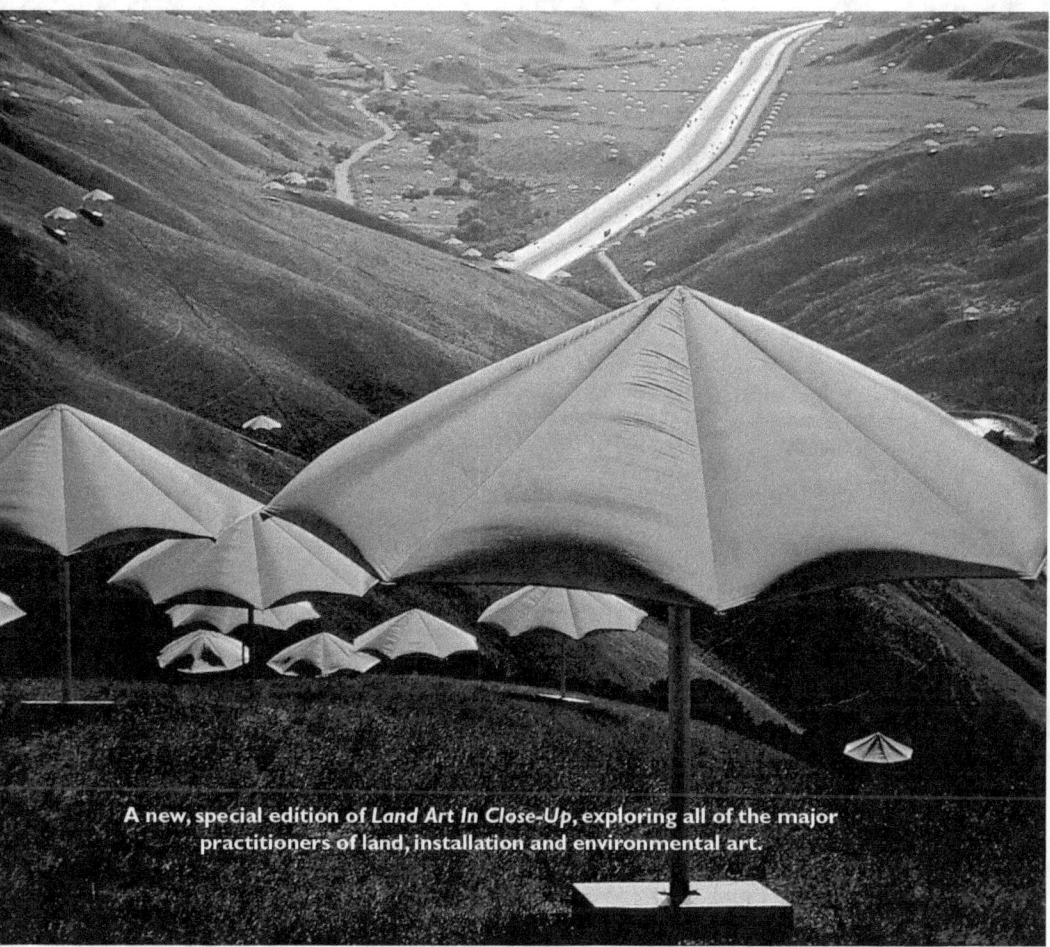

A new, special edition of *Land Art In Close-Up*, exploring all of the major
practitioners of land, installation and environmental art.

Illustrations: 161 b/w, 2 colour. 248 pages. Second edition. Paperback.

Publisher: Crescent Moon Publishing. Distributor: Gardners Books.

ISBN 1-86171-092-5 (9781861710925) £25.00 / $44.00

MINIMAL ART AND ARTISTS

FROM THE 1960S AND AFTER

by Laura Garrard

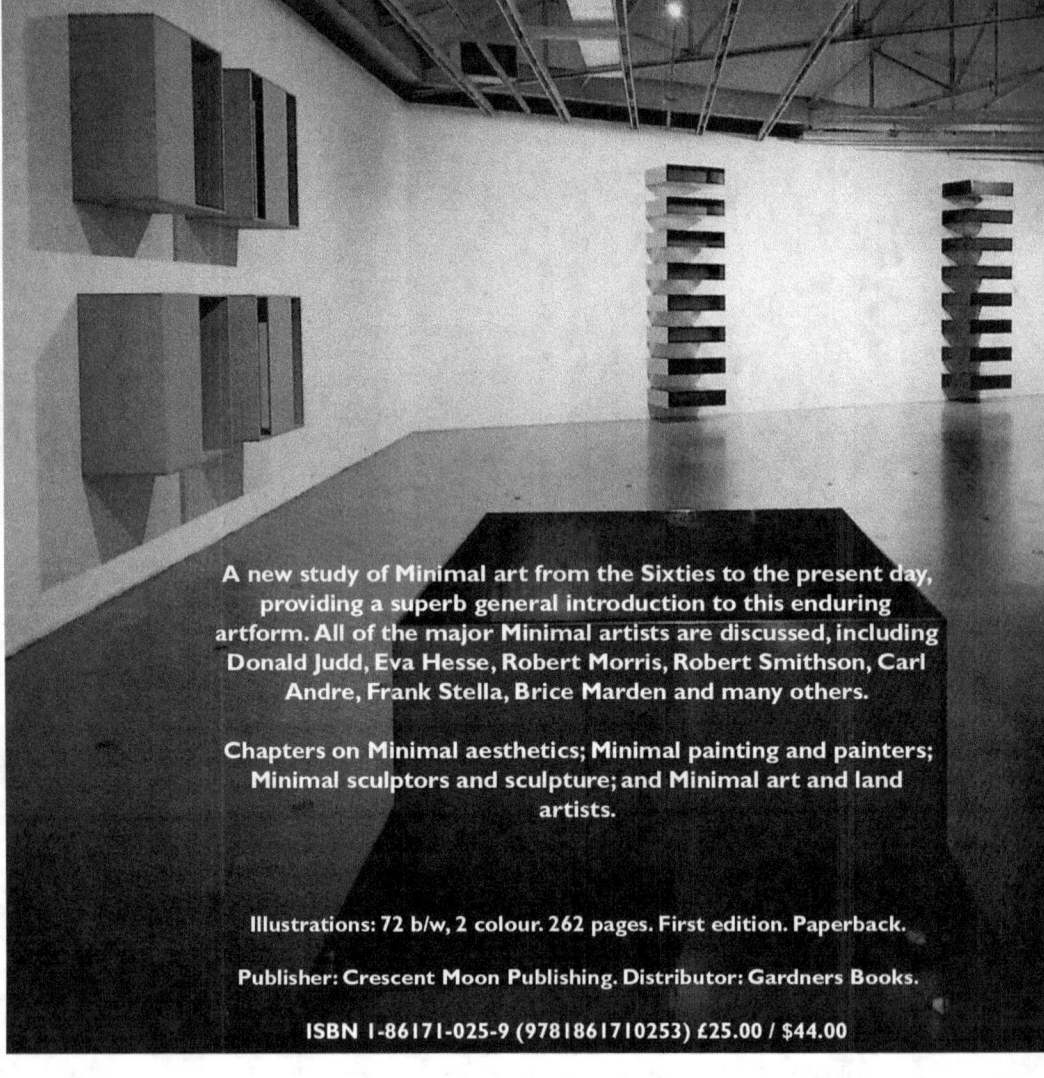

A new study of Minimal art from the Sixties to the present day, providing a superb general introduction to this enduring artform. All of the major Minimal artists are discussed, including Donald Judd, Eva Hesse, Robert Morris, Robert Smithson, Carl Andre, Frank Stella, Brice Marden and many others.

Chapters on Minimal aesthetics; Minimal painting and painters; Minimal sculptors and sculpture; and Minimal art and land artists.

Illustrations: 72 b/w, 2 colour. 262 pages. First edition. Paperback.

Publisher: Crescent Moon Publishing. Distributor: Gardners Books.

ISBN 1-86171-025-9 (9781861710253) £25.00 / $44.00

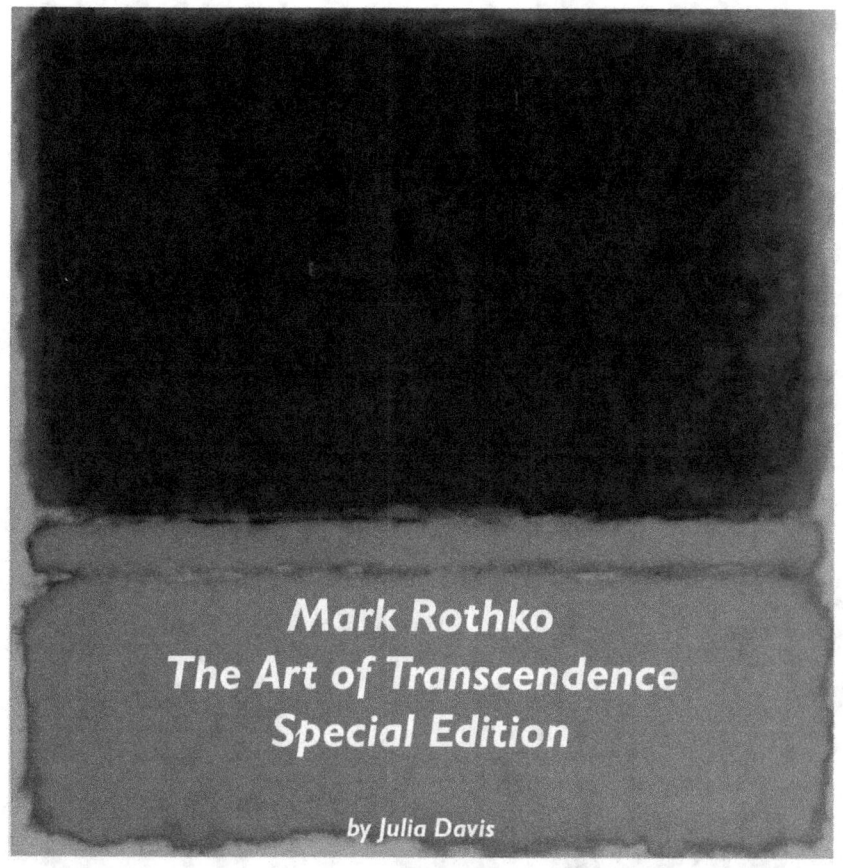

Mark Rothko
The Art of Transcendence
Special Edition

by Julia Davis

Mark Rothko, the American Abstract Expressionist painter, is one of the most widely celebrated of all 20th century artists. His paintings are huge and haunting, marked by themes of tragedy and transcendence. Davis covers Rothko's development from the post-Surrealist semi-figurative works through the radiant canvases of the 1950s, with their floating 'clouds' or 'forms', to the intensity and religiosity of the late mural sequences, the so-called 'Rothko chapels' of Houston, Harvard and the Tate Gallery.

Painters Series   220pp   Bibliography, illustrations, notes   New, 3rd, special edition   ISBN 1-86171-072-0   £14.99 / $26.00

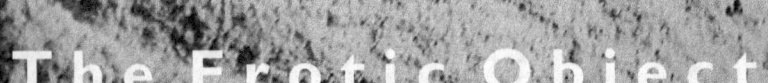

The Erotic Object
Sexuality in Sculpture From Prehistory to the Present Day: Special Edition

by Susan Quinnell

The power of sculpture, form, volume and space is sensitively explored in this wide-ranging study. Featuring discussions of many famous sculptors: Michelangelo, Canova, Rodin, Brancusi, Picasso, Hepworth and Bernini. Many contemporary artists are discussed, including installation and performance artists (Catherine Elwes, Karen Finley, Carolee Schneemann), and women sculptors such as Alice Aycock, Mary Miss, Rebecca Horn, Nancy Graves, Eva Hesse, Kathe Kollwitz and Judy Chicago.
A new special edition, with many new illustrations, a new introduction and bibliography.

(Sculptors Series)   Illustrations, bibliography, notes   326pp.   3rd edition
ISBN 1-86171-069-0   £25.00 / $37.50

THE ART OF
RICHARD LONG

COMPLETE WORKS : SPECIAL EDITION
(HARDBACK and PAPERBACK)

by William Malpas

A new study of the British artist Richard Long, an important contemporary international artist. The most detailed, in-depth
exploration of Richard Long's art currently available.

Illustrations: 48 b/w, 2 colour. 439 pages.
First edition. Hardback and paperback editions.

Publisher: Crescent Moon Publishing. Distributor: Gardners Books.

ISBN 1-86171-079-8 (9781861710796) (Hardback) £60.00 / $105.00

ISBN 1-86171-081-X (9781861710819) (Paperback) £25.00 / $44.00

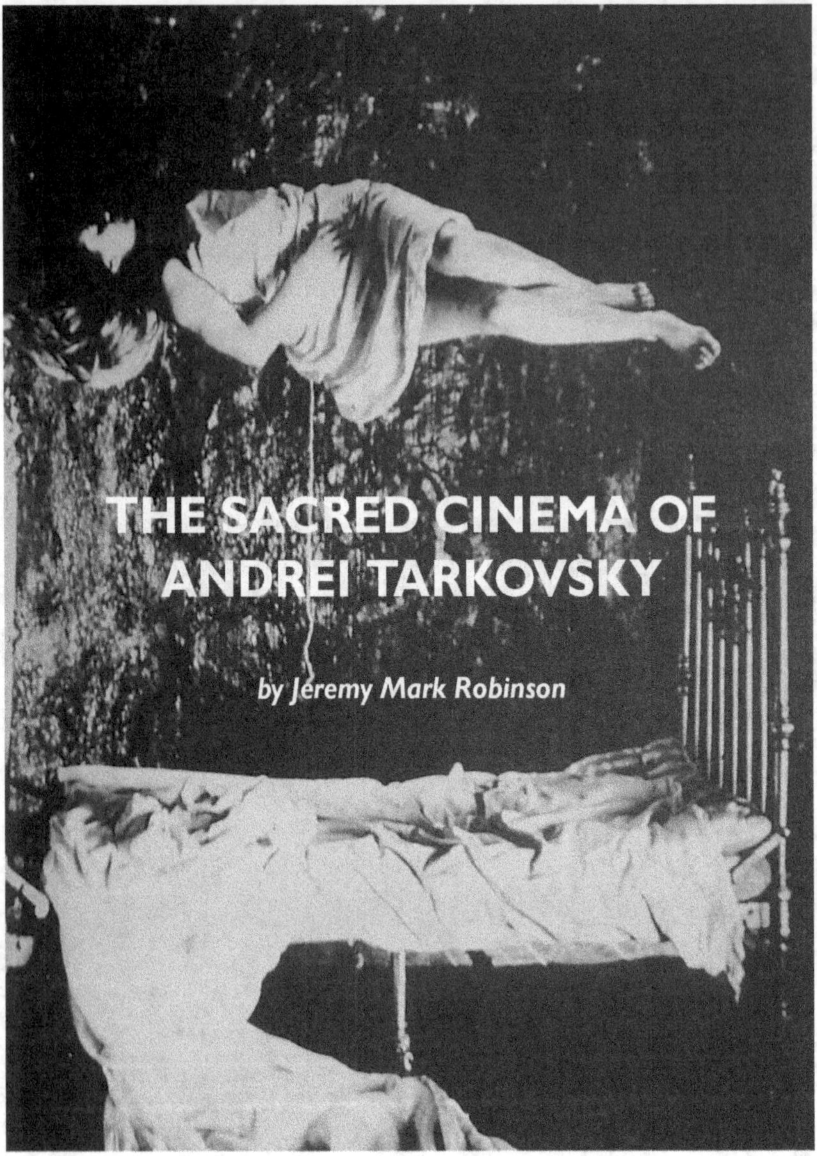

THE SACRED CINEMA OF
ANDREI TARKOVSKY

by Jeremy Mark Robinson

A new study of the Russian filmmaker Andrei Tarkovsky (1932-1986), director of seven feature films, includ-ing *Andrei Roublyov, Mirror, Solaris, Stalker* and *The Sacrifice*.
This is one of the most comprehensive and detailed studies of Tarkovsky's cinema available. Every film is explored in depth, with scene-by-scene analyses. All aspects of Tarkovsky's output are critiqued, including editing, camera, staging, script, budget, collaborations, production, sound, music, performance and spirituality. Tarkovsky is placed with a European New Wave tradition of filmmaking, alongside directors like Ingmar Bergman, Carl Theodor Dreyer, Pier Paolo Pasolini and Robert Bresson.
An essential addition to film studies.

Illustrations: 150 b/w, 4 colour. 682 pages. First edition. Hardback.

Publisher: Crescent Moon Publishing. Distributor: Gardners Books.

ISBN 1-86171-096-8 (9781861710963) £60.00 / $105.00

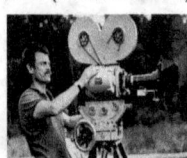